Praise for Surviving the Detour of Divorce

THIS BOOK IS BRILLIANT

"This book reminds everyone affected by divorce that they are never alone. It is absolutely beautiful."

—J. Buchannan, RN, single parent

I HIGHLY RECOMMEND THIS BOOK

"As a divorced Christian, and an L.C.S.W. with over thirty years of experience, I can attest to the importance of divorce survivors having a support system. Surviving the Detour of Divorce is a guidebook filled with inspirational true stories of brave men and women. As you gain powerful insights from their experiences, they will travel with you on your healing journey. The thought-provoking questions at the end of each chapter will guide you on a path of introspection leading you to a place of peace."

—Diane Rose, Licensed Clinical Social Worker

THE STORIES IN THIS BOOK ARE POWERFUL

"No matter our circumstances, the stories in this book are powerful reminders that the Atonement of Jesus Christ can heal one's pain, loss, and suffering if they're willing to lay them at the Savior's feet. Every divorce is unique, as is the heartache for those whose lives are shattered by the experience."

—Abel Keogh, author of *Dating a Widower: Starting a Relationship with a Man Who's Starting Over*

THE BEGINNING OF MORE OPEN DIALOGUE REGARDING DIVORCE

"The heart-felt experiences in this book have helped me through the isolation and transition of my divorce. There may not be a more tragic part of the human experience than a failed marriage due to abuse, infidelity, addiction or other causes. Whether you have suffered from a divorce, a dysfunctional marriage, or know others who have, this is a must-read as it educates and encourages empathy for those who have suffered true and chronic heartbreak."

—Christie Clark, single mom, professional musician

SO INSPIRING

"Surviving the Detour of Divorce reminded me that through the Atonement of Jesus Christ we can be released from our pain; we are not beyond repair."

—Rachel Bromagem, divorced and remarried mother of two

DESTINED TO BE A BESTSELLER

"The painful process of divorce brought Sheri to writing this insightful book. While reading, I found myself saying, 'Yes! That is how I felt' or what I went through. I can identify with feeling like a victim and how detrimental it is to the healing process. I can relate with feeling uncomfortable going to church after being divorced and surrounded by married couples. Thank you for sharing this masterpiece with me."

—Ann Schneider, single mom, assistant teacher

OUTSTANDING EXAMPLES OF HOPE AND COURAGE

"I am not divorced, but I have kids who have divorced and remarried. My adult children are stronger and more appreciative people because of their divorces. This book shows the reader that divorce can be exactly what it claims to be—a detour—instead of a devastating roadblock to a person's progress."

—Noreen Astin, PhD, mother of divorced adult kids

ONE OF MY FAVORITE READS

"I enjoyed this book more than I could have ever imagined. Reading this created a safe place within me to reflect, admire, and grow. A wonderful waterfall of different emotions have come out as I read these true life experiences shared by such a beautiful person and her "carpool" of friends. It is absolutely magical."

—Kathy Bono, divorced business owner

A CATALYST FOR GREATER EMPATHY AND UNDERSTANDING

"Divorce is unquestionably one of the most devastating emotional experiences possible. I know this reality both personally and professionally. Surviving the Detour of Divorce delivers to its readers a paradox of great hope: Divorce can be our life's most powerful catalyst for deep personal growth and positive change."

—Gregory Clark, retired military chaplain

SURVIVING THE DETOUR OF DIVORCE

*My Journey with Christ
and
my Carpool of Friends*

Sheri Rokus

Surviving the Detour of Divorce
My Journey with Christ and My Carpool of Friends
Sheri Rokus

Copyright ©2019
All rights reserved.

No part of this book may be reproduced or transmitted in any form by any means, electronic or mechanical, including photocopying, recording or by any information storage and retrieval system, without specific written permission from the publisher. The scanning, uploading, and distribution of this book via the Internet or via any other means without the permission of the author or publisher is illegal and punishable by law. Please purchase only authorized electronic editions, and do not participate in or encourage electronic piracy of copyrighted materials. Sheri Rokus has asserted her rights under the Copyright, Designs, and Patents Act, 1988, to be identified as the author of this work. This material is neither made, provided, approved, nor endorsed by Intellectual Reserve, Inc. or The Church of Jesus Christ of Latter-day Saints. Any content or opinions expressed, implied or included in or with the material are solely those of the owner and not those of Intellectual Reserve, Inc. or The Church of Jesus Christ of Latter-day Saints.

Sheri Rokus
Roseburg, Oregon

Cover Design: Rebecca Finkel
Interior Design: BookWise Publishing

Library of Congress Control Number: 2019915491

Sheri Rokus
Surviving the Detour of Divorce /Sheri Rokus

Soft cover ISBN# 978-1-7340042-0-5
eBook ISBN# 978-1-7340042-1-2
Audio Book# 978-1-7340042-2-9

10 9 8 7 6 5 4 3 2 1

1.22/2020

Table of Contents

Acknowledgments ix
Introduction xi
Dedication xv
1. Totaled Marriage: Driving Blind 1
2. Finding My Way: The Path of Healing 15
3. Overhaul: Danielle's Diagnosis of the Heart 29
4. Changing Course: Sienna's Struggle 43
5. Stolen Van: Bailey's Unending Faith 55
6. Shifting Gears: Kate's Homosexual Husband 67
7. Blindsided by Agency: The Treks of Two Good Men 83
8. The Crooked Path: Hannah's Detour 93
9. Warning Signs: Hannah's Redemption 103
10. Sarah's Journey: Ben's Life-saving Prompting 115
11. Driving Under the Influence of Pornography: Opposite Outcomes 127
12. Turning on the Headlights of Hope: Auguste's Faith 141
13. Unloading the Junk in the Trunk: Shannon's Awakening 153
14. The Precarious Path: Claire's Unthinkable Sacrifice 163
15. A Fork in the Road: My Test 177
16. My New Carpool Companion: The Unexpected Trip 189
17. Mile Marker Messages 199
Conclusion 201
Bibliography 205
About the Author 207

Acknowledgments

This book is the result of the extraordinary men and women who opened up their hearts and risked being vulnerable. I am profoundly grateful for these survivors who allowed me the honor of recording their divorce journeys. You are all my heroes; thank you.

To my parents; thank you for always believing in me. Always. To my children; please remember that I love you more than words can express. I am profoundly sorry for the pain our divorce caused. You hold a permanent place in my heart. To my husband, Michael; thank you for loving me through it all. To my sister, Janna, who never doubted me or this project; thank you for the hundreds of hours we've spent collaborating. There is nothing quite like "sister love."

Thanks to the following: Precision Editing, especially Mike Glassford; to my critique group, Adelle and Mairi—you are both gifted; to the brilliant staff at the Roseburg Small Business Center, thanks for believing in me; to Rebecca Finkel, the talented and patient graphic designer of my book cover; to Karen Christoffersen from BookWise Publishing, who beautifully crafted the interior design; to Nancy Laney, a fellow author, and unselfish mentor and friend; and finally, to my Beta Readers, (you know who you are); thank you for investing your time, energy, and heart into this project. The quality of this book has soared because of you.

Introduction

According to the National Center for Health Statistics, there is a divorce every 40 seconds in America. That's over 80 divorces every hour. Nearly 50 percent of first marriages, 60 percent of second marriages, and 73 percent of third marriages end in divorce. As a member of The Church of Jesus Christ of Latter-day Saints, the divorce rate among its members appears to be 5 to 10 percent less than the national average, but divorce among people of faith is becoming more prevalent.

This book is intended to give valuable perspective to people of all belief systems who have already been impacted by the tragedy of divorce—which is all of us on some level. I feel compelled to share my own divorce experiences which led me toward a path of personal growth.

My divorce detour began over seventeen years ago. At the time, I seriously questioned how I was going to survive. I interviewed dozens of divorce survivors in my quest for healing. As I traveled with these brave souls, whom I affectionately call my "carpool companions," they inspired me with their faith and helped me face tough questions such as: Was my testimony of God's goodness and the Gospel of Jesus Christ based on having a successful marriage? Was I willing to accept divorce as a trial rather than a judgment? Would I choose to learn from divorce or lose my faith?

Each time I was emotionally stranded, the Lord encouraged me to carpool.

My carpool journey has been an awakening I am excited to share—an expedition that has given my life new purpose and meaning; that is, helping others impacted by divorce to arrive at a place of peace. Each of my carpool companions had a desire to share their stories, to impart new hope and purpose to the inevitable struggle that comes with divorce. These brave men and women had faced a vast variety of issues such as depression, adultery, narcissism, financial challenges, selfishness, same-sex attraction, abuse—verbal, physical, and sexual—along with pornography, and other addictions.

As I invested time in getting to know these extraordinary people, together we realized that our experiences all shared a common thread. We found that lasting and powerful resolution can only be found through the enabling power of the Atonement of Jesus Christ.

There are two sides to every story. Each divorce survivor's experience is told from their own perspective: A one-sided account of two people who divorced. I have chosen to focus on the journey and healing of just one of them.

At the end of each story is a Mile Marker Message that shares what I have learned from my travels with each of my carpool companions. The last page of each chapter has questions with a place to record your thoughts. This is to inspire my fellow travelers to reflect upon their own experiences, because I believe strongly in the power of journaling.

The names in the stories have been changed except for the following: in Chapter Eleven, we learn about Phil and Colleen Harrison, real-life authors who are raising awareness of pornography addiction, and hope for recovery. The names in Chapters One, Two, Fifteen, and Sixteen, have not been changed and reflect my own life's experiences.

In sharing my story, I did not have the luxury of anonymity. My focus was being responsible for my part in divorce and my own journey of healing with others along the way. As a divorce survivor, I still have much to learn.

My life's journey has taught me one thing for sure: Divorce is a detour—not a dead-end.

Dedication

For Michael,

who saw beyond my circumstances.

For Janna,

who believed in me from the beginning.

Chapter One

Totaled Marriage: Driving Blind

We are a statistic. According to Google, the year I was divorced, there were approximately 900,000 divorces in the United States; and *one* of them was mine. America's staggering divorce rate increased because of my shattered marriage—a head-on collision that injured my family and sent our lives on a trajectory to the unknown. Our world as we knew it had ended. Nothing felt familiar as I began to pick up the crumpled pieces of our lives.

How did we get here?

I grew up believing that if I went to church and did my best to keep the commandments, a fulfilling and lasting marriage would be my reward. As a teen, I heard my Young Women leaders encourage my group to make lists of qualities that we wanted in a future husband. My list included someone who was a faithful member of the Church, who honored his priesthood, was a returned missionary, and a good provider. I secretly hoped he would be handsome too.

Armed with my list, I considered myself wise about the men I chose to date and fall in love with. I had a perfect plan—how could it go wrong?

I was the oldest of six children and was close with my parents and siblings. Our family had Family Home Evening every Monday night and learned about the Gospel of Jesus Christ. I was taught the value of education, service, and hard work.

I grew up attending church every week and an hour of seminary each school day during grades 9 through 12. I graduated from high school on the high honor roll, having earned two scholarships. After working all summer to save money, I was ready to launch. Our family, including me and five younger siblings, loaded up the station wagon (wood paneling and all), and headed to Rexburg, Idaho. Even though I didn't have my own car, I was resourceful. I proudly attended Ricks College, walking everywhere in sub-zero temperatures.

After dating up a storm for five months—and dreaming of my happily-ever-after—I got engaged. I had checked every item off of my list. I was prayerful and confident that in God's eyes I was making the right choice. Our engagement lasted three months; long enough to put a wedding together and short enough for the two of us to remain chaste.

Wedding preparations began immediately. My parents had instilled in me the value of thrift, so almost everything would be homemade. As a young girl, Mom was a 4-H instructor and taught me how to sew. Together, she and I made my wedding dress, and then, without missing a beat, she whipped out six purple bridesmaid dresses with very puffy sleeves. In a frenzy, she and Grandma Bessie made eight hundred fruit tarts and some homemade punch for the reception. Our church building gym served as the reception center (and we hoped no one would notice the basketball hoops).

Finally, the day arrived. With temple recommends in hand, my fiancé and I committed our lives to each other across the altar of the temple. We both had large extended families with grandparents, aunts, uncles, and cousins. We invited many people from our church families and many of our neighbors and friends. To my delight, about seven hundred people came to support us at our reception—a sure sign of success (there were even tarts left over).

I was full of the hopes and dreams of youth, and I knew my life as a new bride would be exciting.

I drove full speed ahead toward my ultimate destination, "Marital Bliss." My husband and I looked forward to raising a family and growing old together as we embarked down a road of wonderful adventure; a life, I presumed, of guaranteed joy and eternal happiness.

Fourteen years and four children later, my marriage ended—it was "totaled" beyond repair.

At the age of 33, I joined the ranks of the brokenhearted. I had banked on our idea that our marriage would be forever—for our time on earth and for all eternity. In faith, I lived my life believing divorce wasn't an option for me under any circumstances. When my life detoured, I was forced to think the unthinkable. Divorce would become a permanent part of my identity; a label I perceived as a failure for the world to see—forever.

Divorce happened to *other* families, not mine.

Our marriage had reached a dead-end. Unhealthy behaviors had built up and gotten to the point where I felt unsafe in our marriage. I stayed at home with the kids, and my husband went to a motel.

Five days after separating from my husband, I received a phone call I will never forget. I picked up the receiver and heard my friend, Rachel, on the other end, "How are you?"

Flustered, I responded with a typical, "I'm fine." I wasn't ready to talk about it. Not with Rachel. Not with anyone. I panicked. Holding the cordless phone to my ear, I locked myself in my walk-in closet, surrounding myself with the familiarity of my clothes. I felt vulnerable having the conversation alone, in the expanse of our once-shared bedroom. Somehow it felt safer to be leaning against my wardrobe full of faithful old friends.

Rachel's next words nearly plunged me into cardiac arrest. "I want you to know that of all of the families in our ward, I think yours is the most perfect."

Feeling as if I were strangling on my words, I responded, "Why would you say that?"

"At church during sacrament meetings, I have heard your children bear their testimonies of the Gospel and they speak with such conviction. I wish my family was as strong as yours."

I sank to the floor, landing squarely on the heel of one of my shoes. The physical pain in my backside did nothing to blunt the emotional spiral Rachel had triggered.

I loved this woman; six months earlier, I served as Rachel's Relief Society President. One evening, when Rachel's sick baby had been hospitalized, the two of us visited in the hospital together. Rachel showed strength and conviction as she faced her baby's illness. I admired Rachel so much.

With the phone still attached to my ear, in desperation, I said a silent prayer. *Heavenly Father, what do you want me to say to Rachel? I'm not sure if I'm ready to announce my impending divorce to the world.*

The Holy Ghost brought me a small measure of courage and helped me respond by saying, "My children have been blessed with strong testimonies at a young age to prepare them for trials they'll face in the future."

For a second, I felt thankful that my children had strong testimonies, but my gratitude waned as I remembered our reality. *I would rather my children have weaker testimonies and not be going through this. They are so young, with plenty of time to learn and grow,* I rationalized, trying to bargain with myself. I could not say the word divorce, and at that moment, I would have traded my own situation with almost anyone else's. I honestly couldn't imagine another trial that could be worse than what our family was facing.

We exchanged a few more pleasantries and I hung up. Rachel had no idea. I sat enveloped in a haze of disbelief trying to imagine the shocked look on her face when she found out that our family was part of the 50 percent divorce statistic hanging over America like a storm cloud. The irony of getting the "Perfect Family" label, while Rachel red-tagged her family as somehow inferior to mine, was more than I could take. I had never felt so flawed or imperfect.

Finally, I forced myself out of the closet.

Realizing that others had actually survived their own totaled marriages and were still breathing astounded me. I felt paralyzed and wounded, needing to surround myself with those who understood. But that meant swallowing my pride and telling the world my marriage had failed.

I wasn't ready to come out of *that* closet.

Robotically, I went through the motions of daily life which now included figuring out how to get divorced. I needed a "Divorce for Dummies" manual with chapters on how to keep breathing, provide for my family, keep my kids alive, navigate a new and terrifying legal world, and, oh yes . . . figure out how to stay calm while it felt like my heart was being ripped out of my body. How could I still be alive and feel this much pain? It seemed incomprehensible that the rest of the world could carry on as if nothing earth-shattering had happened.

Several weeks later, the doorbell rang. The kids raced to the door, opened it, and proudly announced, "Mom, it's the missionaries."

Digging deep, I put on my best fake smile and invited them in to visit. We all shook hands and sat down. With excitement, one of the Elder's noticed a picture on the piano. He pointed to a family photo with me and my soon to be ex-husband and our two adorable oldest children. As he did a double-take of me and the kids, he reached into his backpack, and with a look of accomplishment pulled out a pamphlet.

It was the same picture.

Our family was on the cover of a missionary pamphlet for the Church titled, "The Search for Happiness." Surprised to meet the real "Happiness" family in person, they began sharing stories about our pamphlet being passed out by the missionaries. They looked me in the eye and told me how much good our family picture was doing for others throughout the nation. Our happy smiling faces were in every visitor center in North America—and I suddenly despised it.

My family and I could no longer live up to the image we represented.

I politely thanked the missionaries for stopping by and they left. My fake smile immediately vanished as I took the picture down and shoved it into the piano bench. The irony of the situation was too much to handle. Our marriage hadn't been happy for a long time.

All of my hopes and dreams were tied to what that photo represented. I believed that my temple marriage, coupled with printed proof on a pamphlet, guaranteed a forever family. What happened? Silently, I went through my successful marriage checklist:

- *Do my best to be a dedicated wife—check.*

- *Strive to keep the commandments and attend church—check, check.*

- *Try to read the scriptures, fulfill my church callings, and serve our neighbors—check, check, check.*

Wouldn't those actions guarantee a happy marriage?

My extended family had no idea our marriage was unraveling,

and I was determined to put on a happy face. I had become a consummate actress going through the motions of day-to-day life—burying the pain. I was adept at playing the part of a happy wife in public. Not knowing how to love myself or set healthy boundaries, I put on a facade.

Even my best friend, Catherine, did not know I was having marital problems until two weeks before the separation. No one in our ward had a clue. My husband and children were important to me and I did everything I knew how to do to save my marriage, hoping until the very end that we could resolve our differences and our marriage could be salvaged.

When divorce became my reality, I wanted the pamphlet to disappear. The Church owned the copyright to the photograph, so it would pop up in unexpected places. For a time, in the late 90s, our picture was on the front page of the Church's website. The website read, "Welcome to the Official Internet Site of the Church of Jesus Christ of Latter-day Saints." Our family appeared on the right side of the page. When my brother's family went to the Nauvoo Temple dedication, he reported that our picture wasn't just on the pamphlet; it was a *life-sized mural*.

Four years earlier, my Aunt Nancy approached me about our family being on the pamphlet. She worked for the Communications Department of the Church. They were looking for a young family with a blond mom, a brunette dad, and two blond children. That was us. Our height ratio matched the criteria and bam—we were in.

During our separation, I kept asking myself how we could go from literally being a poster family for eternal happiness to a broken family of divorce. Within six months, I went from serving as a Relief Society President to being a single mother, emotionally and physically unable to fulfill a church calling and barely surviving each day.

The next Sunday, I went to church with my secret, hoping no one suspected my new single status. The opening song was "Families Can Be Together Forever." Seriously? My children started to cry and I wanted to scream. As I looked around the congregation, I watched with envy all of the two-parent families sitting together. Pride overtook my emotions as I compared my situation with theirs—they had what I wanted. I was envious of other families who were still intact. Soon, we would be one of those "divorced" families, and that wasn't fair.

My children started sharing the news—and it was big news. *The recently released Relief Society President and her husband are headed for divorce.* A woman in my ward showed up on my doorstep demanding to know if I had been released because of sin. Another sister told me her testimony was based on our "perfect" family. The rumors were flying. Some of the women in the ward I had trusted and served were now judging me—the pain felt unbearable.

I felt like I had been kicked in the gut. But the pain was serving a profound purpose. From that moment on, instead of judging broken families as people who couldn't quite get it together, or made bad choices, I suddenly discovered that they were some of the bravest people on the planet. My paradigm had completely shifted—and that was another humbling experience.

The new Relief Society President and I visited together to discuss the situation. With permission from the bishop, I addressed the sisters in Relief Society. I tried to find my voice, and I reassured the sisters that I had served them worthily. From the depths of my soul, I expressed sincere sorrow about the confusion our divorce was causing. As I acknowledged their frustration because of not knowing the personal reasons for the divorce (which I never shared), I expressed my deep love and concern for each of them. I concluded my talk by bearing my testimony.

My new life as a single mother began by overcompensating. I was driven by a determination to protect my children's tender little hearts. Day and night, I knocked myself out trying to be a super mom. Families are designed to have two parents in the home for good reason—parenting is tough. Working around the clock, I tried to make up the difference for their heartache, desperately wanting to take away their distress.

How did I get here?

Growing up, I wanted to do everything right. To be, well, perfect . . . as if that were humanly possible. My desire to be baptized was strong, but I was afraid of making mistakes.

Before my eighth birthday, I would lie in bed praying I would die in my sleep. I was a very serious seven-year-old. Being fully accountable for my sins after I turned 8 caused me great anxiety. I didn't believe I would be strong enough to keep my baptismal covenants. Longing to be near my Heavenly Father, I believed I had to be perfect to go to heaven.

I missed the memo about the Atonement of Jesus Christ.

As a little girl, an unrealistic perception of the nature of God set me up for some tough life experiences. I struggled to see God and Jesus Christ as individuals loving and supporting me, in spite of my weaknesses. Instead, I lived in fear of disappointing them. I didn't realize that they were compassionate beings, full of mercy and grace, with a perfect plan to help me be successful—no perfection required. It would take years for me to accept this principle.

Because of my core beliefs, I entered marriage demanding perfection of myself. Being young and idealistic, I assumed that doing my best would be enough to work through any relationship problem. Determined to be perfect, I focused on my flaws and allowed others to do the same. My misguided beliefs hurt our marriage; they hurt me.

Rather than relying on my Savior and accessing the power of His Atonement each week during the sacrament, I punished myself for not being perfect. I did not understand that perfection lies in working toward wholeness.

While striving to be perfect, it became apparent that this mindset would be difficult to maintain in marriage—but I was determined. Reprimanding myself to have more faith and try harder didn't help. I continued to be a pleaser, putting impossible expectations on myself, sacrificing everything for the greater good of my marriage and family. While living under this constant pressure, I ignored some of my most basic physical, emotional, and spiritual needs.

It was confusing. I had been taught a true Christian principle—to lose myself in service.

My mother is a beautiful example of being Christ-like. She serves my father and me and my siblings with endless energy. Mom's heart is too big for her body and I have often been the blessed recipient of her never-ending love. She fulfilled her church assignments, cooked, sewed, canned food, remodeled, is a devoted wife, raised six great kids, and served her parents.

There wasn't anything Mom couldn't do—except take enough time for herself. I rarely saw her meet her own needs when I was growing up. As a mature woman, my angel mother has grown to love and value herself. She has recognized that she needs to love herself as much as she loves everyone else. This was a revelation for me.

During my marriage, I lived like I had watched my mom do in my formative years. Self-love and self-care were unfamiliar concepts. I struggled to find a balance between meeting the needs of others and loving myself. My identity was so wrapped up in the roles of wife and mother that I'd forgotten I was a daughter of God—and deserved to be treated as one by others and myself. The Holy Ghost kept trying to teach me to love myself, but I was a slow learner and ignored His teachings. In my mind, "Love thy neighbor as thyself" meant "Love thy neighbor and lose all sense of self."

My family came from a long line of pioneer ancestors who had crossed the plains, braving every storm until they marched triumphantly into the Salt Lake Valley—or dropped dead trying. I was a Clark, and Clarks didn't give up. I would persevere and sacrifice, doing whatever it took to succeed and have a happy family.

Looking back on my life, I see some of the pride that led to our downfall. Always feeling pressure to look the part, our family lived in survival mode. Determined to live up to the "Happiness" label that described our family on thousands of pamphlets circulating throughout North America, I was too afraid to ask for help when I was in trouble.

In envy, I watched my siblings with their spouses and children. Instead of being happy for them, I was mad that they had what I wanted. I didn't view myself as prideful—but I was. I had always viewed pride from the top down, looking down at others. I didn't understand pride from the bottom up. My feelings of envy, anger, and jealousy stemmed from my own pride.

The constant reminders of our failed marriage were taking a toll. When I thought I couldn't take any more, Heavenly Father intervened.

One morning, while visiting my children's school counselor, I told him how hard I was trying to make it all work. It felt like

I was killing myself attempting to make up the difference for my children's pain from our divorce. That wise counselor looked me in the eye and said, "Sheri, there is only one Savior, and guess what—it's *not* you. Let the Savior do His job."

That statement would change my life. Accepting that I couldn't save anyone, not even myself, was a new concept for me. Who did I think I was anyway? I had not been relying on the Savior to save my children. Saving myself and my family was Jesus Christ's job and I hadn't allowed Him to do it. I hadn't been ready to access the spiritual help available from above.

Divorce is a trip—a road trip. It is shared with family, friends, and most importantly our Heavenly Father and Jesus Christ. Our support system, or carpool of friends, expands when our journey detours. As we navigate together, we share Mile Marker moments that remind us we are not alone.

Through this tragedy I learned: I don't have to be perfect to be loved by God.

Mile Marker One: Let the Savior Do His Job

Today, seventeen years later, tears of joy and gratitude have often accompanied my prayers as I thank God for my siblings and other families who have *not* endured the tragedy of divorce. I have become more aware of the challenges they face that I don't. A divorced person doesn't corner the market on trials—none of us get through this life unscathed.

Divorce has given me a new vision of the world from an unexpected vantage point. Instead of divorce being a negative label, it is now a critical part of my life's journey. I have learned painful, yet priceless, lessons. As I embark on a journey of self-acceptance and love, I'm learning to reclaim my power as a valued daughter of God.

As I carpooled with other divorce survivors, I gained intimate insight into their suffering. Today, I remind myself more quickly that there is always so much more to every story.

The infinite Atonement of Jesus Christ applies to infinite divorces; and every kind of devastation in between. The Savior is merciful to divorce survivors. He has descended below every level of emotional, spiritual, and physical pain. Our sanctifying submission to God's will, especially when it doesn't make sense, releases pride.

While navigating my detour of divorce, for a time I couldn't see light at the end of the tunnel. As I turned toward God, I prayed to feel my Savior's love. I sought answers from the Spirit and realized the Lord was sending me a clear message: With Christ, I was enough. But it took years for me to actually believe it.

Now when I look in the rear-view mirror, I see how I was carried beyond my own capacity. The light of the Savior fueled my journey through the dark tunnel, empowering me to face something I could not have survived on my own. I realized that I can't look back in healthy ways until I begin to move forward.

When I divorced, the greatest journey of my life began—the journey to know my Savior.

As I look back on my experiences of divorce I have learned to:

- *Be happy for others with intact marriages—avoid pride from the bottom up.*

- *Let the Savior do His job.*

- *Accept that I don't have to be perfect to be loved by God.*

Questions

As you read about my struggle with pride, do you have any insights about the role that pride may play in your own life? In your divorce? Or the divorce of someone close to you? Can you be happy for others with intact marriages?

_____
_____
_____
_____
_____

How have experiences related to divorce given you the opportunity to get to know Jesus Christ in new ways? What can you do to invite Him into your carpool? Are you letting the Savior do His job? Why or why not?

_____
_____
_____
_____
_____

Heavenly Father and Jesus Christ love you perfectly as you are. Make a list of your strong and unique qualities. If Jesus was writing the list, what do you think He would say about you?

_____
_____
_____
_____
_____

Chapter Two

Finding My Way: The Path of Healing

Facing the first weekend alone without my kids was unbearable. I had one probing question demanding an answer: Would I live through this biting pain? It was worse than the excruciating back labor during my daughter's delivery. And this time, there would be no quick end to the suffering or reward on the other side.

My mother-guilt was paralyzing.

Many fathers and mothers surely feel the same despair as they go from seeing their children every day to every other weekend and one night a week or less. Parent-time never feels fair, and the difficult feelings that surface over these issues can be consuming.

Not only did I have to deal with my fragile feelings, but the anxiety of my young children was crushing. They loved both of their parents and could not fully understand what was happening in their lives. How do you tell a one-year-old crying for her daddy that she can only see him every other weekend and one night a week? How do you explain to your children that because of their parent's choices, neither parent will always be there for them? Now a judge has the final say on when you see your kids when you can't come to an agreement yourselves.

As a young exhausted mother, I had fantasized about having a weekend without my children. How wonderful it would be to meet my own needs for 48 hours. How ironic that it was so terrible when it actually happened.

Soon the divorce papers were signed and the children's first weekend with their father arrived. The doorbell rang and my heart sank.

And they were gone. Just like that. I managed to keep breathing, barely. I escaped reality in front of the TV, watching one movie after another. I was emotionally unable to use the time away from my kids to rejuvenate like I should have. Depression and guilt consumed me. After three movies, I couldn't find the energy to walk to the bedroom. I fell asleep on the couch.

With no children to be my alarm clock, I woke up late on Saturday morning—with no purpose. As if someone had pushed the "on" button of the remote control, I dressed, grabbed my purse, and walked outside to my van. My brain and body were barely connected as I climbed in, buckled my seatbelt, and turned the key. Suddenly, I was on the road; I didn't even remember backing out of the driveway. The van seemed to be on autopilot, compensating for how lost I felt inside. A traffic accident ahead jarred me into reality. I felt like I was driving blind.

I suddenly felt an urgent need to connect with someone who had survived divorce and lived to tell about it. Determined to find answers through another person's story, I found myself in front of a Christian bookstore. Unwavering in my mission, I needed to know I was not alone.

There had to be other survivors.

As I walked through the door of the bookstore, it felt like everyone was staring at me and knew that I was broken. I walked deliberately down the aisles, perusing the displays. The inviting smell of fresh books helped me breathe and began to calm the near-panic that had been my constant companion for endless days. With new found hope, I combed the shelves.

Self-help books describing how to have a happy marriage seemed to leap off the shelf. Titles about "Family Happiness" slapped me in the face. The search became arduous, and with each title the sting grew stronger. I felt frantic. Where were the divorce books? Where was a clerk? When I located Katie, a perky red-headed employee with freckles and an enormous smile, I asked for help and she did a search. Unbelievably, there were no books on divorce. How was that possible? Was I the only human on the planet that wanted to read a Christian divorce book? In a sing-songy voice, Katie was overly apologetic as I clenched my teeth and fought back tears.

In stunned silence, I headed to the parking lot, trying to ignore the empty car seats as I climbed inside my minivan. As I drove, powerful emotions began to overtake me. Suddenly, I veered to the side of the road, pulled over, and sobbed—the torrential rain kind of sobbing. Inconsolable, I questioned God, begging Him to take away my pain. Was the Atonement of Jesus Christ really real? Did He actually have the power to heal my wounded heart? Did His suffering include me? My kids? Did He really understand the depths of my guilt and grief?

In agony I waited—I could barely breathe.

If I had been the victim of a random car shooting, someone would have noticed and called 911. An EMT would have rushed to my side, called for backup, and stopped the bleeding. I would have been given CPR and an oxygen mask, been taken by ambulance to the hospital, and then rushed into surgery. Eventually, my hospital room would have been filled with beautiful flowers and lovely cards. Others would have surrounded me with care, compassion, and no judgment.

As I sat sobbing in my van, there would be no ambulance rushing me to the hospital. No EMTs checking my vitals or giving me CPR. No oxygen mask to help me breathe. I had not received any flowers or cards. On the outside I looked just fine—but I was gravely injured.

My soul was bleeding on the inside. It was hemorrhaging.

When the tears ran dry, I leaned on the door of the van for support. Desperate for relief, my thoughts went heavenward—there was nowhere else to turn. I said a silent prayer, begging God to take a portion of my pain so I could bear it. I continued to pray; a life and death kind of prayer.

Slowly, I began to breathe. As my heart opened, thoughts of my Savior flowed into my mind. Finally, I began to allow the peace of the Holy Spirit to enter my soul. He assured me that Jesus had carried me through the fog of the previous months. Without His help, life would have been impossible to manage. The Lord *had* been navigating for me, but I hadn't recognized it.

At that moment a powerful desire filled my being. I was propelled by a new purpose—I would be the one to write a divorce book. I would find other survivors who were willing to share their stories. Someday, divorced men and women like me would *not* go home empty handed when they found themselves alone, driving blind to a bookstore.

As time moved forward, I tucked my resolve in the back of my mind. Being strong enough to someday write a book was unfathomable. There would have to be a lot of healing first. I never imagined it would take seventeen years. At that time, I wasn't capable of helping other survivors. Whether or not I would actually survive was still in question.

The month our divorce finalized, my former Relief Society counselor called and ordered me to sit down. Her voice sounded grave as she asked me to open the December *Ensign*. She asked if I had read it and I hadn't—with four small children I barely had time to go to the bathroom. Miraculously, I found the magazine, flipped to the right page, and saw my smiling face next to my soon to be ex-husband and two oldest kids staring back at me. Our family picture was front and center, part of an *Ensign* article called, "Family Happiness," by Marlin K. Jensen.

That was a bad day.

In protest, I wrote a letter to the Church headquarters explaining that the "Happiness" family was no longer happy—and newly divorced. A few weeks later I received a response in the mail. The pamphlet was used on such a wide scale, the Church would keep it in circulation until it would be updated. My heart landed in my stomach. The ongoing reminders of our failed marriage were like that horrible song that gets stuck in your head—it wouldn't stop playing.

One day, I literally fell on my knees in front of my children. I was mentally, physically, and spiritually exhausted. The kids were fighting and I was at the end of my sanity. After a few minutes, the kids calmed down, wondering why Mommy was crying on the floor. My children wanted answers I couldn't give them. As a mother, I yearned for the kind of wounds that would heal quickly with a Band-Aid and a kiss.

Life had drastically changed. My husband was a good provider and I was a stay-at-home mom. I was busy taking care of my home, family, and serving the sisters in my church.

Suddenly, I became a single mom of four young children, ages 1 to 11, with a baby in diapers, trying to meet their physical and emotional needs. It felt like I was stuck in a bad dream that I could never get out of.

Desperate for help, I turned to a friend for a priesthood blessing and he graciously agreed. He laid his hands on my head and pronounced the Lord's will. The blessing he gave me literally changed my life. He quoted the following verse in the Bible from Paul to the Hebrews:

"But call to remembrance the former days, in which, after ye were illuminated, ye endured a great fight of afflictions . . . Cast not away therefore your confidence, which hath great recompense of reward." (Hebrews 10:32, 36)

Just like the Hebrews, our family was enduring a great fight of afflictions. My friend reminded me, through the voice of the Lord, that if I placed my confidence in Him, my family would be rewarded. In the blessing, I was told how to manage my self-talk. Whenever I began to feel discouraged, I was admonished to rededicate myself to the Lord.

With renewed faith, I submitted my will to the Lord's. Day after day, I would literally say the words in my mind or out loud, *"Lord, I'm rededicating myself to thee. Please help me get through the next minute, or ten minutes, or hour."* Every time I said those words in faith, I received spiritual strength and power through the Holy Ghost.

Changing my self-talk changed my life.

The blessing encouraged me to study the Bible. As I did so, my desire to understand the life and mission of Jesus Christ increased. I yearned to know Him as a person; His likes and dislikes—His personality. What would it be like to be around Him? I wanted to further access the enabling power of His Atonement in my life, and to be imbued with His grace.

Additionally, I increased my study of *The Book of Mormon*. Jacob 3:1 became my favorite verse. During my darkest hours I read this verse hundreds of times:

"But behold, I, Jacob, would speak unto you that are pure in heart. Look unto God with firmness of mind, and pray unto him with exceeding faith, and he will console you in your afflictions, and he will plead your cause, and send down justice upon those who seek your destruction." (Jacob 3:1)

When we look to God, and pray in faith, He promises us three things:

1. *He will console us in our afflictions.*
2. *He will plead our cause.*
3. *He will send justice upon those who seek our destruction.*

These powerful promises were available to me the minute I reached out to the Lord. God doesn't promise us that if we go to church, keep the commandments and do our best, we will ride off into the sunset, experience "Marital Bliss," and never get divorced. Instead, He promises to console us *during* divorce, plead our cause, and send justice upon those who seek our destruction. The promises were a healing balm to my wounded soul—*when I allowed them to be.*

When my life fell apart, I felt decorated with personal medals of failure. It was as if all of my family and friends had shown up, uninvited, to ceremoniously witness the demise of my marriage. I felt like announcing, "There will be a press conference afterward, folks. Just bring all of your most personal, humiliating questions for me, and we'll have a Q & A."

When someone loses a husband or wife to death, family and friends surround the grieving spouse offering love, assistance, and support. There is usually a funeral or a life celebration. Cherished friendships may grow stronger. In most cases, the spouse left behind is treated with tenderness, compassion, and no judgment.

There is no public grieving ritual for divorce.

Divorce is uncomfortable for everyone involved and no one knows how to behave. No one. Insecurities are unleashed. Members of your support system may now be unavailable, such as your former in-laws and friends you shared as a couple. Family members and friends may want and even demand justification for your divorce. The grieving parties are thrown into a world full of unsolicited advice, blame from others, and a loss of treasured relationships.

Every death requires a grieving process, including the death of a marriage.

All marriages begin with hopes and dreams. No marriage was ever *all* bad, which makes divorce confusing. Often, the most significant losses are the ordinary rituals such as having a movie buddy, sharing inside jokes, religious practices, vacations, and couple friendships. Joint finances and credit scores are affected. Household responsibilities such as home and yard routines are dissolved. What happens to family pets? The loss of emotional and physical intimacy can be shattering. For couples with children, deprivation of consistent contact with your children can be devastating.

During the darker times of divorce, the devil would bait me with discouragement. At times, I allowed him to edge me away from the light down unsafe roads. When I looked at my life through the rear-view mirror, without the companionship of the Savior, I was on a one-way street headed for disaster. I was in emotional and spiritual danger.

One day, I was heading down the freeway and was angry about my divorce. I wasn't just angry; I was fuming. As I chose to fuel my negative momentum, soon I was going twenty-five miles over the speed limit. Screaming sirens shifted me back into reality, along with a big fat speeding ticket. My negative momentum was out of control and I had no clue I was speeding.

My negative thoughts continued to gather momentum and soon I was heading down a dangerous road (the speeding tickets were adding up). I needed to practice putting on the brakes to my negative self-talk and make a U-turn. I had to consciously switch gears. Then, with focused attention, I could begin driving my thoughts in the opposite direction.

One way to guarantee negative momentum was to play the "What If" game. "What If" I hadn't gotten married young? "What If" I had set better boundaries? "What If" I had chosen to love and value myself? When I was at a critical turning point, instead of focusing my thoughts on Christ, I focused on my failures. I learned an important lesson—there's no winning at "What If."

Fixating on an ex's misdeeds will drive anyone straight to the top of the pride cycle. I know, I've been there. For a time, I chose to be a victim, focusing on blaming my ex-spouse. This angry cycle didn't change him, the negative momentum changed me. Blaming an ex-spouse is like getting bit by a poisonous snake and seeking revenge by killing the snake that hurt you. Consumed by revenge, you don't realize the poison is killing *you*—and you forget the antidote.

When dealing with the complexities of divorce, it's astounding that more people don't go insane. Without some self-checks I probably would have. In order to shift gears with my self-talk I needed to slow down and ask myself, "Who's driving me? The Spirit of God or Satan?" Often, I needed to come to a complete stop, repent, and focus on changing *me*. With help from the Lord, I began monitoring my self-talk and paying attention to the power of momentum.

Negative self-talk is really self-torture.

Switching gears doesn't mean you have to read scriptures for ten hours. You could listen to music, watch a movie, or give service. Keep going until you feel the energy shift. Sometimes, when the load is too heavy, the only thing that shifts the momentum is going to sleep. When you wake up, begin again, and purposely choose the conversations you will have with yourself.

There's no way to get to the bottom of what happened in a divorce. There is no bottom. Choosing to pay attention to what we're actually telling ourselves about ourselves, our former spouse, our parent guilt, or our past wounds is enlightening—and sometimes shocking. Dwelling on the negative becomes a habit. We choose to pick at our wounds until we're bleeding again.

How do we find the motivation to care? By caring about how we feel.

My friend, Glenda, has quit worrying. She said, "When I'm worrying, I'm not happy, and I want to be happy." This sounds so simple—yet, so hard. Glenda is a wise woman who cares about how she feels. We can soothe ourselves by becoming better managers of our inner voice.

The key: Reach for thoughts that bring a feeling of relief.

Allowing yourself to feel relief when things aren't fully resolved will be one of the greatest gifts you can give yourself. Remember, your thoughts create your feelings. They aren't created by your circumstances. Shifting our thoughts will shift negative momentum. A situation may be too far gone for us to make *it* better. All we can do is choose thoughts to make *us* better.

Finding a support system is critical in working through grief. Many survivors don't have supportive families to turn to. I am very blessed to have loving parents who stood by me during my divorce.

My dad is a retired social worker and he guided me through hundreds of hours of pro bono counseling (and rants). My sweet mother came to stay with me and the kids for six weeks. I can never repay their kindness and unconditional love; I don't take my parents for granted.

During the first week of my separation, my sister, Janna, literally came to my rescue. A few months earlier, she, too, had gone through a divorce. She took time off of work, climbed on a plane, and spent a weekend ministering to me and my children. I will never forget her kindness and unconditional love.

Even with family support, I was crashing. Finally, I was ready to really invite Jesus Christ into my carpool. Hoping that His guidance would provide divine direction, I began to focus on Him. I learned that wounds from divorce heal faster when our journey includes the Lord; but it's up to us. The gift of agency allows us to work through our issues at our own pace.

As I worked toward healing, the Lord sent additional friends—carpool companions to accompany me on my path. These divine appointments indelibly imprinted upon my mind and heart the power of love. Through these friendships, my faith in Jesus Christ grew stronger. Each carpool friend traveled with me until I had safely arrived at the next Mile Marker of my journey. Some friends traveled with me for a season; others continue to travel with me to this day.

Each of these friends generously shared their uniquely personal divorce stories with me in their own words. They, too, had a desire to make a difference for others. These survivors had allowed the pain from their past to serve a divine purpose. As they willingly opened their hearts, I accepted this sacred trust, and together we put their unique journeys on paper.

These survivors faced a myriad of issues such as mental illness, narcissism, personality disorders, anger, same-sex attraction, and dysfunctional communication. Some endured the betrayal that comes from shattered trust. Both men and women in my carpool have been wrenched by the devastation of adultery, emotional affairs, addictions, and broken covenants. Money problems and selfishness have wreaked havoc. Many survivors and their family members have endured unthinkable abuse: physical, emotional, and sexual.

We all needed the Savior to do the job that He alone could do—save us.

I am forever changed because of the remarkable men and women who joined my carpool. As a fellow divorce survivor, I am honored to share their inspiring stories of hope and the power of the human spirit. They taught me an extraordinary lesson: I was single—but not alone.

Mile Marker Two: Give Way to the Rocky Road of Grief

I have learned that it is critical to allow yourself to grieve—fully. During varied stages of grief your self-talk will be different. Remind yourself that your heart needs time to heal, just like a physical wound. For a time, my self-talk was dedicating myself to the Lord. Other than that, I could not tell myself anything else positive. Ask Heavenly Father to help you find the self-talk that works for you.

Anger is part of grief but can become an obsession. Many divorce survivors obsess over being wronged by their ex. They will not reach for feelings of relief until their former spouse has apologized and made restitution. That kind of expectation eliminates their free will and creates frustration. Those thoughts generate negative momentum that is powerful and pointless.

When my mother-guilt became paralyzing, thoughts of love were the most honest and soothing answer. I told myself how much I have always loved my children and will continue to love them. When I was ready, I acknowledged that for a time, I truly loved my former husband.

My cousin, Greg Clark, a fellow divorcée and retired chaplain in the Air Force, shares these profound words: "I believe that Satan would have us believe that the very real love, faith, and trust we extend in 'failed relationships' is all a complete waste. Ironically, it is this very kind of patient and unconditional love that we extend in our marriages, irrespective of the outcome, which will ultimately exalt us. Don't give up on love, for pure love is of God."

The following exercise helps me to mentally switch gears. Make a list of negative feelings. On the other side, write down the opposite of each statement and turn it into a positive.

Negative Momentum	Positive Momentum
I'm a failure because I'm divorced.	Some marriages aren't meant to last.
I've made so many mistakes.	I did my best. I will become emotionally and spiritually healthy.
I've damaged my children.	I love my kids. They are resilient.

Through my experiences with grief I have learned to:

- *Allow myself to grieve fully; I am on my own healing path and time frame.*

- *Recognize the momentum of my thoughts; reach for thoughts that bring relief.*

- *Replace feelings of guilt with expressions of love for myself and my children.*

QUESTIONS

The grieving process is deeply personal. A divorcée, or close friend or family member affected by divorce, may go back and forth between stages. Where are you in your own grieving process? How can you educate yourself regarding grief?

_____
_____
_____
_____
_____

How has the momentum of your self-talk affected your healing process in positive ways? In negative ways? You are in charge of your feelings. How can you care more about how you feel?

_____
_____
_____
_____
_____

We are commanded to love (remember we are not commanded to trust). How can expressions of love or kindness for yourself, your children, or even a former spouse affect your self-talk?

_____
_____
_____
_____
_____

Chapter Three

Overhaul: Danielle's Diagnosis of the Heart

Since childhood, Danielle and I have traveled many bumpy roads together. She is a vibrant, attractive woman, with curly brown hair and naturally thick and beautiful eyelashes. She divorced six months before I did and was sensitive to my needs. The week of my separation, she dropped everything and came to my rescue for the weekend. She arrived with self-help books, yummy snacks, and toys for the kids. Danielle was able to look at both sides of a situation. When she divorced, her broken heart led her to diagnose the issues in her former marriage. In turn, she inspired me to perform a similar diagnostics on my own issues and to be accountable for my part in divorce.

Danielle's Story in Her Own Words

I've heard of someone's first love being compared to a heroin high. There is nothing quite like it, and it's next to impossible to duplicate that first experience. Jeff was my first true love; he was my everything. I would have walked through fire for that man.

Jeff and I met through a mutual friend, Abby. She and I had been friends for many years and were roommates in college. After graduation, I met Jeff at Abby's family home and we immediately connected.

After a few meaningful conversations and several dates, I told Jeff I loved him. That had never happened to me before. I know I sound cliché, but I really felt like we knew each other before we came to earth and we were finally reconnecting. Our bond was immediate, and powerful.

Jeff and I had great communication. He was very loving and respectful. However, in spite of his good qualities, he could be emotionally unstable at times and had several unresolved issues from his childhood. He grew up in a home with parents who slept in separate bedrooms. There was a lot of unresolved family conflict.

Jeff was eight years older than I and had quite an interesting past. Prior to us dating, Jeff had been divorced twice. His first wife was a girl he had dated in high school. They were young when they married, and she had a change of heart a couple of years into it. His second wife had serious mental health issues and a very complicated past. After her repeated affairs, he left. Jeff also struggled as a teenager when his first love, Andrea (Abby's sister) had broken up with him. This left him wounded. Additionally, Jeff had experienced a major loss with the death of his father.

I dated Jeff on and off for two years before we married. We had many differences to work through. Jeff was inactive in the Church and he didn't keep the Word of Wisdom. When I became overwhelmed with our differences, I would pull away. I was very confused about our relationship and needed some space, so I decided to go on a mission.

Six months into my mission, I started having health issues and needed anti-depressants. I felt the Spirit whisper that I should marry Jeff and I came home early from my mission. That was a very traumatic time dealing with so many emotions and all of the questions regarding my early return. Gratefully, my parents were amazingly supportive. They weren't thrilled about Jeff's situation or his past, but they were completely respectful of my decisions and my journey.

Jeff and I got married six months after I came home from my mission. We continued working through our differences—it wasn't easy. Throughout our marriage, Jeff was always supportive of my involvement in the Church. True, I would have liked to have a husband who was active in the Church. But I loved Jeff. He went through a period between the second and third year of our marriage where he thought I would be happier with someone active in the Church. He insisted that we separate and we did for a short time.

After living apart for nine months, but continuing to have contact, it became clear to both of us that our relationship was progressing. We moved back in together and began to start saving money for a house. The next year, after the separation, things started going really well. We began our fourth year of marriage with the purchase of a lovely rambler-style home with a gorgeous view of the valley and a swimming pool. This was a big accomplishment for us, and I started feeling much more secure in our relationship. The holiday season was beginning, and it was so much fun to be in our new house. It felt like it might be time to start having kids.

For no apparent reason, Jeff started acting stressed out and defensive toward me. I sat him down and insisted he be straight with me. What was the matter? Jeff confessed that Andrea, his first love, had started emailing him. She claimed she'd had an epiphany that she was still in love with him. Jeff was honest and told me about Andrea's emails. He was struggling emotionally and felt his unresolved emotions for her starting to take control. Jeff was opening up his heart to her and said he couldn't help his feelings.

The reality of what he was saying made me feel weak. I remember feeling as if all the blood drained from my face and upper extremities. I tried not to panic and did my best to show him love, acceptance, and support. After all, he had given me the same kind of love and acceptance with my own personal weaknesses.

Jeff's unhealed wounds with Andrea were a much greater force than I had realized, and he crumbled under the pressure. He described to me how he felt emotionally thrown and confused. Andrea was his first love, and he had been heartbroken when she had called off their relationship. He told me he loved me, but explained that he had never gotten over Andrea. I reassured Jeff of my love, and that I wanted him more than anything, but he had to decide what he wanted.

Deep down, I knew that Jeff loved me, and that he was confused. From my perspective, things had been going so great. I couldn't understand what was happening. I started feeling as if I were driving blind, hitting black-ice on the freeway, spinning completely out of control.

For the next ten days, Jeff was deciding between me and the other woman. I wanted to share the horror of what was happening with someone—anyone. But, I hoped things would work out, so I kept it to myself. At least Jeff was being honest and sharing his feelings with me. Then the bomb dropped. He said he felt like we needed to get a divorce because of his feelings for Andrea.

It felt oddly peaceful in that moment, like the Spirit was saying, yeah, you should get a divorce. But the calm feeling quickly turned to panic—I loved my husband.

Jeff decided to go to Arizona to spend Christmas with Andrea so he could figure things out. With almost no warning, my husband was on his way to visit his first love. I was a complete mess. On Christmas morning, I woke up alone in our beautiful home. Mustering up the courage to go see my extended family, I spent the day holding back tears, while watching my siblings with their spouses and children.

I tried to focus on breathing through my pain and panic. Looking back, that was probably the worst Christmas of my life.

Between Christmas and New Year's Day, Jeff called me on the phone. He was frantic, saying he had made a terrible mistake. While in Arizona, he and Andrea had been intimate, and he told me that it felt wrong. He promised to never do it again. Jeff appealed to me, begging me to take him back. During the phone conversation, I sensed how emotionally distraught and confused he was. He was haunted by the unresolved feelings he still harbored for Andrea.

I was confused. Jeff had been honest with me, yet he had cheated on me. I loved him and was willing to do anything to save our marriage. Part of me wanted to have him back. The other part was in shock. I felt shaky, but I wanted to be hopeful. Up until that point, he had been open and honest with me. Ultimately, our communication gave me hope that we could figure things out together.

Jeff was worried that I wouldn't really forgive him and would hold the affair over his head, but he said he was willing to try. This was completely uncharted territory. I felt as if I had emotionally gone off the grid. I was afraid to get angry; afraid that my anger would push him away.

Claiming he loved me, Jeff returned from Arizona, resolved to work things out. Afraid that my family would never fully accept him, he bravely wrote them a letter asking for acceptance and forgiveness.

In January, Jeff began therapy. One day, he showed me a handout the therapist had given him describing different reasons husbands struggle with their wives. He then proceeded to point out several of my weaknesses. It felt like a contest between his mistress and me. Cruelly, he acted like he might give me a fighting chance and was interested in having me win. It was hurtful and confusing because he clearly had lost sight of the sanctity of marriage.

In order to mitigate his guilt, Jeff started picking me apart and made a laundry list of my faults. He didn't like my nose and suggested I get a nose job. He often compared me with Andrea, sometimes in my favor, giving me compliments on my intellect, talents, and physique.

Halfway through January, I logged into Jeff's email account and saw emails from Andrea. It was alarming, although I didn't read anything inappropriate. I confronted him, and he said he was working through it the best way he could.

Several weeks later, Jeff had a business trip to Arizona. I was petrified, because that's where Andrea lived. But, the business trip had been scheduled several months before, so it seemed legitimate. During the whole trip, he called me constantly to reassure me and let me know what he was doing. He seemed so attentive.

It's mind-blowing how it can feel as if your spouse is being completely honest with you and then find out he's been lying. It's actually amazing how easy it can be for someone to lie. A few weeks later, Abby called me at work and dropped the final bomb. She said, "Danielle, I am having mixed feelings about calling you. My husband said I should stay out of it, but I feel like we need to talk. Jeff and Andrea are being intimate behind your back."

When I got off the phone with Abby, I paused—sixty seconds of horror. Then I called Jeff and confronted him. It was a relatively calm but firm conversation, and he confirmed the facts. My worst nightmare became a reality; he had chosen Andrea over me and was continuing to have an affair. I hung up the phone and drove home in a haze.

Robotically, I did the things I needed to do to end the marriage.

I packed and moved out that weekend. Within a week, I had the divorce paperwork filed. When I wasn't at work or bawling my eyes out, it felt as if my heart was wrenching with the greatest anguish imaginable. Jeff had made a choice to be dishonest and unfaithful; our marriage had not been perfect, by any means. But I had signed up for it, emotional difficulties and all. And now, I could not trust him anymore; and I could not live under those circumstances.

I've read about the stages of grief: denial, anger, bargaining, depression, and acceptance. I spent the next two years of my life mostly in depression, with a big dose of bargaining. I missed Jeff and wanted to be with him. He was my life and letting him go was like cutting off my air supply.

It took several years before I allowed myself to get angry. Looking back, I was so sad and weepy. Most of the time I was too tired to feel anger, just sadness. He had been a great husband in so many ways. Whenever my friends or family criticized Jeff, I would defend him. In time, I hoped we could somehow come back together and regain a relationship of trust. I knew how emotionally wounded he was by the whole thing, and how it truly hurt him to hurt me. But the unhealed wounds from many years before had a stronger pull on him, and he couldn't hold his moral character together.

After our divorce, Jeff's relationship with Andrea grew rocky. He would periodically contact me (every four to six months) and say he wanted me back. I would see him once or twice, hoping he would start making better choices so we could get back together, but he always reverted to Andrea, especially since I made it clear that I wouldn't be intimate with him.

During this time, I experienced panic attacks, which were new and terrifying. I have a family history of depression and medication was the only way I could get through my day. Thank goodness for psychiatrists. Additionally, I had a trusted therapist, along with many true friends.

In order to repair my broken heart, I began to diagnose my situation. I read a bunch of divorce books. In one of the books, it talked about how both parties needed to accept responsibility for their choices. At first, I felt victimized and couldn't see how any of my actions were wrong, or that I had any responsibility in our divorce. It was Jeff and Andrea's fault, not mine. I truly was the victim and nothing I had done warranted their terrible behavior toward me.

However, looking back, I now see my limited perspective. There were things I needed to learn in order to move past the role of "victim," which actually felt comfortable, to a place of real healing. During those tumultuous times, it was hard to understand why things happened the way they did. Plus, I still felt so much desire for Jeff. I loved him all along and couldn't turn that off overnight. So, I reached out to my Savior, Jesus Christ. I studied my scriptures with more intent. I did a lot of journaling. I listened to uplifting music. God sent several people to help me, to buoy me up, and to bring joy back into my life. I began to recover and have more balance in my life.

A year later, I took the next step toward repairing my heart. Slowly, I began genuinely trying to understand Andrea. I wasn't excusing what she had done. Instead, I tried to understand her choices. In her late teens, Andrea had faced great turmoil of her own. Her mentally ill father had left her mother and siblings after subjecting them to years of abuse. Andrea had been through some truly terrible things. I tried to put myself in her shoes.

It was humbling to realize how I had been blessed in ways that Andrea lacked. I had a wonderful family to whom I could go for emotional support. My dad gave me many blessings of comfort.

When I thought of Andrea's family, I knew she didn't have the same resources. Her family could be very volatile.

During this fragile period, I was called to teach Relief Society. It seemed that nearly every lesson I prepared was a hugely trying, emotional experience for me. Yet, I was given perspectives integral in helping me try to understand Andrea's situation. That repair work was hard, humbling, and cleansing. After all, she was the other woman.

I realized that Andrea and I both needed the Atonement of Jesus Christ, equally. She was a daughter of God and my fellow sister.

I felt the Lord guiding me carefully during that time and giving me the perspective I sought. Looking back, it was quite amazing. I'm so glad I stayed active in the Church. It helped me come out much further ahead in my healing schedule.

Three years later, I had done a lot of processing. True repair work on my heart meant that I had to be honest with myself and start seeing things more clearly. I had not been wise in choosing a marriage partner. When I married Jeff, I knew he could be emotionally unstable at times. He didn't have access to the blessings that one can receive from faithfully going to church meetings. Jeff wasn't blessed with the same family support and encouragement I had been given to help him make righteous choices; but I chose him anyway.

Looking back on our past together, I made peace with my choice and forgave myself. I learned many valuable lessons from Jeff and from the whole experience. For a time, I was dearly loved by my husband and we grew from our experiences together.

After my divorce, there were several emotionally unstable guys who had similar weaknesses to Jeff with whom I had relationships. They were not active in the Church, either. Why did I put myself through that again? Why didn't I immediately realize that I was making bad decisions in my post-divorce dating? I remember thinking, *what's wrong with me? I'm a smart girl, right?* I've since realized that it takes time to make changes. I was instinctively drawn to those types of men because it felt "normal." Now, I have grown enough on my own to recognize how to identify and correct the poor choices I made in the past.

It has taken years of being an obedient member of the Church, calling on trusted friends for support, and going through my own experiences, to realize how the choices I made contributed to the problems in my life. This recognition and further repair work has enabled me to forgive myself. Had I held onto my anger and my belief that I was the victim, I could have ended up in the same situation again. Through hard work and patience, I allowed the Spirit to touch me and teach me. These were tough lessons.

Finally, I reached the place where I could easily resist the type of man who wasn't good for me. That change didn't come overnight; it required lots of practice and patience. After the divorce, I desperately wanted to get married again, but the Spirit guided me to do what was best for me, not just what I wanted. Realizing my part in the situation was a big step, Heavenly Father knew I needed plenty of time to learn how to make good decisions on my own, even against my most sincere pleadings for a husband.

While I was single, I finished a Bachelor's degree in communications. Studying and learning about healthy communication helped me figure out the psychology of my past and aided my healing process. I learned about being in a healthy and assertive relationship.

In codependent relationships, people tend to be either passive, giving into the other person's needs by being respectful to them and not to themselves, or aggressive, by being respectful of themselves, but not showing respect for the other person. The healthy way is to be assertive. In this type of communication, you show respect for yourself *and* the other person by listening and setting healthy boundaries. It's important to be fair, firm, and friendly.

During this time, it seemed like the phrase "a broken heart and a contrite spirit" would often jump out at me as I read my scriptures and listened to church talks. Part of my repair process meant turning to the Lord and allowing myself to be fully vulnerable to Him. I've heard it said that the Savior can only reach us through the cracks in our broken heart. I have experienced this. It is painful, but the healing is real.

After seven years of being single, I finally fell in love with a wonderful man who had also been through a similar divorce situation. Heavenly Father had truly prepared us for each other. It kind of blew my mind. After a year of dating, we were married in the temple, and these last ten years have been so sweet. I truly feel like he will be mine forever.

Occasionally, even after being happily married, I would have dreams about Jeff. Wondering if I would ever find closure, I shared these dreams with a counselor. She asked me an interesting question. "Have you released Jeff from all guilt and shame?" Wow. That question stopped me in my tracks. No, I hadn't. I realized that deep down I had been hoping that Jeff's dishonorable decisions still haunt him, and I was secretly glad.

I took this to the Lord and He helped me fully cleanse my heart toward Jeff. I also pictured myself handing over my judgment of Andrea to the Lord. I began to honor her life's journey more fully as well. My counselor said that when my heart was fully cleansed,

I would feel toward Jeff and Andrea as I would toward a brother or a sister.

One night, I had a dream about them. We were all happy and peaceful, living in harmony. I had sincerely doubted that I could ever have those feelings about Jeff and Andrea, but I know that the Savior has carried me through all of my pain to the other side. It has taken many years, but it has happened, and I am truly grateful for the time Jeff was in my life.

Mile Marker Three: Seek a Diagnosis and Repairs from the Master Mechanic

Danielle is a beautiful example of a humble divorce survivor taking ownership of her part in a failed relationship. Jeff had the affair, not Danielle, yet she willingly diagnosed and addressed her own issues. She did a tremendous amount of introspection, study, and the emotional work needed to overhaul her heart. Instead of remaining a victim, she asked the Lord for His help in her healing.

Failure to diagnose the issues surrounding a divorce postpones healing. Most of us dread this process because it requires humility.

Danielle's unyielding commitment to deal with her own issues showed me a new path that led to healing through the Savior. Danielle encouraged me to step up and be responsible for my life circumstances. Performing a diagnostic on my own failed marriage was difficult, but carpooling with Danielle made it doable. Her example propelled me forward.

Imagine your car is broken down on the side of the road. You desperately want to get it running but you know nothing about fixing cars. Instead of allowing a mechanic to take your vehicle to his shop for repairs, you decide to sit on the side of the road in the broken-down car, refusing to surrender your vehicle to the professional.

You claim you want to get your car running, repeating your plight to others, but you don't have the tools or expertise to fix it.

Still, you refuse to get out of the car.

Holding onto the past is like clinging to the broken down car. Until we surrender our hearts to the master mechanic—our Savior Jesus Christ—we are powerless to heal from the past and let it go. Regardless of how broken we are, God is still the God of miracles and He wants to help us recognize them in our lives. We may be in desperate circumstances, having a totaled marriage and a broken heart, but we are not beyond repair. Our Savior is the Master mechanic. He has all of the tools to repair our hearts and has paid the ultimate price for us to be re-built.

Carpooling with Danielle taught me that:

- *Being remarried doesn't erase the pain of a previous marriage and divorce.*

- *Without diagnostics and repairs, our future relationships are at risk.*

- *As a victim, it's important to heal and rise above having a victim mentality.*

Questions

If you are married or divorced, to what extent did you understand your spouse's weaknesses before you married him or her? If you could go back to your pre-marriage self and give yourself advice, what would it be?

_____
_____
_____
_____
_____

If you are divorced, what is your perspective today on why your marriage ended? What was your part? Your spouse's part? Ask God for help in making a divorce diagnoses. Pray for a greater perspective.

_____
_____
_____
_____
_____

If you feel like you have been a victim to an ex-spouse, is it important to shed having a victim mentality? Why or why not? What repairs are needed to help you heal and re-frame the past?

_____
_____
_____
_____
_____

Chapter Four

Changing Course: Sienna's Struggle

I liked Sienna the moment I met her. She had long brown hair, caramel-colored eyes, and a caring smile that radiated kindness. After our introduction, I immediately felt like she had a genuine interest in my well-being. Destined to be one of my carpool buddies, we became friends. As we continued our travels together, she shared her story of loss and redemption. Sienna's struggles with church attendance after divorce resonated with me. It was difficult attending church where I was surrounded by two-parent families. Because of my struggles with perfectionism, I spent my time in meetings feeling guilty about my divorce. I allowed myself to feel so bad about my situation, that I too questioned why I even went.

Sienna's Story in Her Own Words

As a child, I loved visiting Temple Square in Salt Lake City, Utah. I gazed at the gates and imagined going there with my future husband. By the time I was a senior in high school, I had spent most of my life dreaming of going to the temple to be married. I believed in the concept of eternal marriage and that the union between husband and wife does not end in this life, but can go on forever.

One night of bad choices had temporarily locked me out of the temple. Now pregnant, I looked at the same beautiful and ornate temple gates, realizing my dream was gone and my heart was broken.

My boyfriend, Ken, and I got married, and as the years went by we had four children. We decided we wanted an eternal family. We set a goal to be sealed in the temple so we could be together forever. It took a lot of effort, and the repentance process was harder because of the choices we had made, but it was worth it. Ten years after we were married, my dream finally came true, and our family was sealed in the Salt Lake Temple for time and all eternity.

Shortly after our temple sealing, my husband's job took us back East. We were both sad to leave Utah, but we grew to love the people in our new city. We both served in the Young Men and Young Women programs of the Church. Unexpectedly, after several years, Ken was offered a job back in Utah. In spite of the close friends we had, we felt this would be a great opportunity for us. Ken would make more money, and we would live close to our families again.

We decided it would be best for me to stay with the kids and sell the house while Ken started his new job. I felt like we were close as a couple and we'd grow closer together through the experience. As time moved on without a buyer, I found myself feeling alone and discouraged caring for four small children by myself. After six months, the house had not sold, and our long distance marriage was strained.

One day, I was shocked to find many members of my church standing on our doorstep. They had buckets of paint and tools to fix up the house. Accepting their help was humbling. I didn't realize that others knew about our struggle. With their service, I found renewed hope that the house would sell.

After all of our hard work, we still didn't have a buyer. Desperately wanting my family to be together, I didn't think I could take any more. When I was on the verge of losing hope, my agent called to say there was an offer on the house. I found out later that a miracle had taken place on my behalf. Another real estate agent had heard about our family being separated and bought our home so I could be with my husband. This random act of kindness was completely overwhelming. I was so grateful.

When the house was finished, Ken flew home to sign the papers. When he arrived, he seemed like a complete stranger. He had been totally active in the Church until he moved to Utah for his new job. While in Utah, he quit attending church and was living a bachelor's life. I didn't know who he was or what to say to him.

Something had shifted in our relationship. Ken wouldn't communicate with me and I felt totally in the dark. We were finally together, but I felt alone. The children and I packed our bags and moved to Utah to be with Ken. Things were strained and silent between us; it was agony. A month after the move, he walked into the bedroom and said, "I want a divorce."

He moved out, and I gave up.

I hit a fork in the road and went into a deep depression. I'd been abandoned by my husband, my supposed eternal companion, and I felt lost. The wonderful journey I thought we were taking had drastically detoured, and I was broken. In time, we divorced, and I became a single mother.

As a newly divorced Latter-day Saint, I went through a time when it was extremely painful for me to go to church, but I continued to go for my kids. After my divorce, I allowed myself to feel "less than" others who had been able to hold their marriages together. Because I didn't value myself, I struggled with making friends and was overly sensitive.

I reached a critical turning point and began searching for answers. Why was I going to church? Why should I go and listen to lessons about forever families when my family had fallen apart?

Often, I felt bad after attending my meetings; I didn't see the point.

Satan started planting seeds of doubt in my mind. I allowed him to convince me that working so hard to get to the temple had not done me any good. Because my marriage had ended, it felt like the last ten years of effort were a total waste of time. I threw everything away I had once believed in. It seemed as though not caring was easier, and at that point, I did not care.

While trying to enjoy my rebellion, I headed down the wrong road. When I started online dating, I began looking for guys on the Internet who would validate my new choices, making a point to *not* meet members of The Church of Jesus Christ of Latter-day Saints. I tried to meet anyone who would convince me that the way I had been living in my former life as a member of the Church was wrong.

Looking back, I realize how vulnerable I was. While dating, I agreed to meet men I knew nothing about. I met one of them alone at his home in the mountains. The guy was full of deception and lies—he could have been a rapist. He claimed to be a life coach, saying he was going to "help" me. He took advantage of where I was in life. He was a tour guide, and he knew I loved the outdoors. I remember thinking, *if he is who he says he is, I'll be alright.* It's hard to believe I was that trusting. I could have been killed.

Later, I took another wrong road. I met Tim on the Internet and began dating him seriously. Within a short time, we decided to live together. He was very controlling and abusive, always wanting me to pawn off my kids. He desperately needed me, but not in a healthy way. Not wanting to be hurt again, I thought his need for me would keep him from breaking up with me. I was blind—I couldn't handle that kind of pain. Over time, I began to see my blindness, recognizing that he wanted to stop my growth and control me. Finally, I asked him to move out.

At the same time, I met Matt. He was one of "those" members of the Church of Jesus Christ of Latter-day Saints, but something about him drew me to him. He opened my door for me and asked about my kids. As we continued dating, he told me to take my time; he truly cared about my needs and the needs of my children. He was different from the other men I had dated. It irritated me at first, but his patience and kindness attracted me to him. Matt recognized that my kids were an extension of me. He was respectful of healthy boundaries—but I wasn't healthy. It kind of bugged me that he respected me.

Deep down, I felt I didn't deserve respect.

My feelings of insecurity stemmed from my dad leaving when I was a small child, age 2, and then my former husband leaving me.

I had been blinded by an all or nothing perspective. In my eyes, I had taken one road—gotten married in the temple—and look where it led me. I'd been abandoned, alone, and miserable. At that point, I couldn't see the personal value of keeping the commandments and going to the temple. All I could see was my failed marriage. I was so devastated because of my divorce that I missed seeing the importance of all of the experiences in between.

In spite of my choices, I wanted my children to grow up with values and go to church. Ironically, I was still attending services with them every Sunday. Something was drawing me there that I could not figure out and I was confused. Finally, I realized that I didn't know if the Gospel of Jesus Christ was true, and I needed to gain my own personal testimony. If the Church was true, then maybe there was a purpose to my life.

My kids went to their dad's house for a three-week visit, so I took the time to go back to Illinois and visit some early church history sites. I was ready to decide for myself what I believed. Also, I wanted to see my old friends back East who loved me.

Matt joined me on the trip. He was going to ask me to marry him, but realized I wasn't ready. My spirit was in turmoil and I felt bad for him because I was not very attentive. I was lost, determined to find out who I really was, and to know for myself if the restored Gospel was true.

The Sacred Grove in Palmyra, New York, was a highlight for us. Miraculously, we were alone in the Grove for twenty minutes. As we sat and pondered, we both felt a lot of peace. We walked into the visitor's center to look around. Once inside, I noticed a lady that kept staring at me. She came over and started a conversation and said, "Why are you here?"

"I'm here for me," I told her. "I need to figure out the Church."

She touched me on the arm, and I experienced an intense feeling of being cradled. The feeling was so overwhelming that I started to cry, so I went to the restroom. She talked to Matt while I was gone. When I came back, we chatted for a few more minutes, and then we filled out a card with our contact information.

After leaving the visitor's center, we got lost and ended up in front of the temple. I know Heavenly Father was guiding us. While we looked at the temple, I told Matt about the warm feeling I experienced while visiting the kind woman. When we got home, I began to feel a lot of peace about the Gospel. The Holy Ghost was working with me and I was finally becoming open to the influence of the Spirit. I was at another fork in the road.

I was confused and afraid to trust men—including God.

Deciding which way to turn was a battle. Two weeks later, I got a call from the visitor's center, and the same sweet lady was on the phone. She said, "I felt impressed to call and tell you that the man you were with was very genuine." Her call was out of the blue. I was looking for confirmation that Matt was a man I could trust.

As I continued to seek answers, I counseled with my bishop. He told me he thought Matt was "genuine." There was that word again. Matt had a light about him that I recognized later as the Spirit of the Lord. He was so patient with me. Matt talked to the missionaries and told them that I had a lot of questions about the Church.

We started having the missionaries come over for dinner. During the visits, we had a lot of fun talking and they didn't pressure me. One day, they asked me to kneel with them and pray to find out if the Church was true. At first, I was ornery because I was embarrassed to say a prayer, but I finally agreed. As I prayed, I felt like I was going to cry. For the first time in a long time I felt like I had a church family. I realized that I had lost my ex-husband, but I had a ward family all along.

I had never been alone.

Another time, I saw Matt standing in the doorway and a strong feeling of emotion came over me. I was reminded of the temple covenants we had both made previously. When I went to church, I realized that the sacrament was for me. It was personal.

Matt proposed two weeks later. After a six month engagement, we married. Being married to someone who merely holds the priesthood, versus someone who honors and lives it, makes all the difference. It is a miracle. We have now been married for ten years. There's a totally different feeling in our home living with a righteous priesthood holder. We have a combined family of seven children ranging from ages 13 to 19. In spite of the craziness of having seven teenagers, there's an underlying feeling of peace that only comes from living the principles of the Gospel.

I have reflected upon the day I was sitting in front of the temple gates, pregnant and devastated that I wasn't worthy to be married in the temple. I realized that I was a child preparing to have a baby.

Now as a woman, I understand that God has times and seasons. We need to do things according to His steps and in His way. We bring some of these painful trials upon ourselves. Now I truly feel like a mother because I'm doing things the Lord's way. As a result, I'm receiving the sweetest compensatory blessings in return. I got to walk through the beautiful temple gates with my son, the baby I conceived out of wedlock, who is now a young missionary preparing to teach people about the Gospel.

My son is choosing not to skip the steps Heavenly Father has given to us as gifts. He has his feet firmly planted on God's straight and narrow path. To see him making good choices, doing things the Lord's way, is an extraordinary blessing. As I sat in the temple looking across at my son, the joy I experienced was beyond description. What a precious gift to have a son who loves the Lord. As a missionary, he may be able to help prevent a young woman from making the same mistakes I did.

Each principle of the gospel is a stepping-stone on the road leading to eternal life.

When you start to skip the daily steps that keep you heading in the right direction—such as prayer, scripture study, temple attendance, and service—you're going to get off the path. It's much harder to find your way back to the road, but the stepping stones are still there.

Looking back on my life with perspective, I realized that my foundation wasn't strong. It wasn't the temple or the Church that failed me. I made the choices that propelled me off the Lord's path. Marriages that will last for our time on earth and for all eternity require two willing and forgiving people. For a time, I failed myself and my children. I remember thinking, *Oh well, if I die, I have nothing else going for me.* When you are completely lost, you lose hope.

One time in church, it hit me really hard that I was not worthy to partake of the sacrament. When I made poor choices, I put myself in a position where I had lost my ability to choose. The choices I made took my agency away, and I handed it over to Satan.

The adversary convinces us that the commandments are restrictive when the opposite is true. Taking the high road gives us the freedom to be guided by the Holy Ghost and be spiritually safe. Years earlier, when I was working toward a temple marriage, I was going through the motions. Now, I realize that temple worthiness is an everyday thing. In my first marriage, I was dreaming so much about what I wanted, a temple marriage, that I didn't live in the now.

Mile Marker Four: Take the High Road

I met Sienna when I had reached a fork in my own road. Going to church was something I had done without question my entire life until I divorced. It was difficult being surrounded by two-parent families. Like Sienna, I struggled with insecurity and the judgment I felt from others. Once I realized I needed to mature spiritually and figure out for myself why I go to church, I decided to try an experiment. Each Sunday, I set a goal to focus on the Savior and ponder the meaning of His Atonement during the passing of the sacrament and the sacrament prayers. I love the personal invitation for each soul to keep sacred covenants. I cherish the extraordinary promise at the end of the sacramental prayer on the bread as follows:

"Oh God, the Eternal Father, we ask thee in the name of thy Son, Jesus Christ, *to bless and sanctify* this bread to the souls of all those who partake of it; that they may eat in remembrance of the body of thy Son, and witness unto thee, O God, the Eternal Father, that they are willing to take upon them the name of thy Son, and *always* remember him, and keep his commandments which he hath given them, that they may always have his spirit to be with them. Amen." (Moroni 4:3, emphasis added)

In this prayer, we covenant to: 1. Willingly take upon ourselves Christ's name; 2. Always remember Him; 3. Keep His commandments; 4. And receive the promise: we may *always* have His Spirit to be with us.

Why is this promise so valuable? When we speak by the power of the Holy Ghost, *we speak the words of Christ.* In *The Book of Mormon*, Nephi confirms this truth:

"Angels speak by the power of the Holy Ghost; wherefore, *they speak the words of Christ.* Wherefore, I said unto you, feast upon the words of Christ; for behold, the words of Christ will tell you all things what ye should do." (2 Nephi 32:3, emphasis added)

The sacrament is a deeply personal ordinance. A piece of bread is broken for each person and a cup of water is poured. When we partake with a sincere heart, we are participating in a step-by-step process of becoming holy. Sienna inspired me to determine why I go to church, and I did: I go to worship my Savior.

From Sienna's experiences I learned:

- *To focus on my need to repent instead of my perceived judgments from others.*
- *The sacrament helps me renew my covenants and receive the words of Christ directly.*
- *I go to church to worship my Savior.*

Questions

Have judgmental comments from others affected your church worship or attendance? In what ways? Is it possible that your perceived judgments of them have caused you to be judgmental?

_____
_____
_____
_____

The sacrament is deeply personal. How can you more fully focus on the Savior and receive more personal revelation during this ordinance? Pray for guidance and record your impressions.

_____
_____
_____
_____

If you are currently attending church, why do you go? How do you prepare yourself to worship?

_____
_____
_____
_____

If you are not attending church, identify and record the reasons. Where can you turn for peace?

_____
_____
_____
_____

Chapter Five

Stolen Van: Bailey's Unending Faith

The first time I saw Bailey at church, I wanted to meet her. She looked like an angel with gorgeous green eyes and long, wavy hair. Her countenance glowed. When we met, it felt like reconnecting with an old friend. I was newly divorced and dealing with custody issues. Bailey was separated from her husband, hoping to reconcile. We had much in common. As our friendship grew, there were times it felt as if the lives we'd both imagined had been stolen and someone else was driving. In Bailey's case, not only had someone taken over the steering wheel, they had literally stolen her van.

Bailey's Story in Her Own Words

I joined the Church of Jesus Christ of Latter-day Saints as a ten-year-old child. When I saw the missionaries walking down the street, I felt compelled to follow and ask them to come back to my house. When they taught me the gospel, I knew immediately that the Church was true. I received a testimony of *The Book of Mormon* before I finished reading it.

Since my baptism, my faith has been tried a great deal. That is one of the reasons we're here—to be tested. Nevertheless, I have spent most of my life worrying about basic needs. As a young girl, my house was the one other children's parents did not let them go to because of the drugs and the men who hung out there. It was uncomfortable inviting friends over to play. I didn't feel accepted in my ward or at school.

Having the Holy Ghost was a gift of rarest value to me. His companionship helped me through the unspeakable trials that plagued my youth.

At age 21, I served a full-time mission for eighteen months. I was blessed to have my mission paid for by relatives and my ward family. When I arrived home, and later married in the temple, I was still young at learning how to value myself. It has taken me years to begin to understand and believe that I am of infinite worth—in spite of my parents' mistakes and my own. I'm still in the process of learning to love myself and believe that I am worth loving.

During my first marriage, I found out that my husband, Alex, and I were several months behind on the mortgage payments. The news was devastating. I prayed and fasted for financial miracles and increased my temple attendance.

Then I found out that we were not current on our tithing. This put us in a very tough spot, so we counseled with our bishop. With his help, Alex and I decided to pay our tithing. I have always believed that if you put the Lord first, including His command to pay tithes and offerings, you could never go wrong. Although the Lord answered my prayers for help in a magnificent way, there was not enough money to bring us both current on tithing and our house payment. We lost our home—but I have never regretted the decision to pay our tithing. The Lord has truly opened the windows of heaven for my family.

At the same time, it came to light that Alex had been struggling with a very serious addiction. After going to counseling, and making many attempts to work through our issues, Alex and I separated. It seemed as though I would get past one hurdle only to have another one placed on my path. We continued going to counseling and working together financially, hoping to save our marriage. As a family, we attended church and other functions together.

Our best friends, Troy and Elizabeth Tate, invited us to their daughter's baptism, followed by a potluck dinner at their home in the country. It was awkward attending functions with my husband, but I was looking forward to this special event.

The morning of the baptism I woke up feeling angry and upset; my spirit was in turmoil. My feelings didn't make sense. This was a blessed and happy occasion. As I pondered the situation, I realized that the only other time I had felt similar anguish was several years earlier when my life was in grave danger. Was I feeling that way because I was in danger? Or was the adversary trying to keep me from attending the baptism? Confused, I prayed for an answer and received no direction. I told Heavenly Father that if it wasn't right for me to attend, He would need to make it clear. Again, I prayed for answers and God was silent. I made the decision to go.

After the baptismal service, we traveled to the Tate's home. We were enjoying a nice meal when our friend Troy emerged from the barn with a horse that was very tall and muscular, a huge animal. Troy offered to give the children rides. Immediately, I started having an uneasy feeling and wanted to skip anything involving the horse and go home. My husband and kids were having a great time and wanted to stay.

Excitement filled the air as the guests lined up for rides on the horse. Alex got in line with our two youngest children. Shortly, with Troy's help, they were mounted on the saddle. Alex got distracted and started visiting with other people. Feeling panicked, I headed toward my children and walked along the side of the horse, holding my son's hand. The horse knew I was there and I was careful to not touch it in any way.

While our kids enjoyed the ride, Troy guided the horse around the side of the house. As we turned, he took the corner too close, not allowing enough room for me and the horse. Without warning, the horse reared up, bumped into the side of me, and kicked me sideways.

I flew twenty feet in the air.

The impact of my body hitting the ground was excruciating. Three of my ribs were broken in ten places. One of my lungs was punctured and was filling with fluid. I was gasping for breath. My liver and adrenals were badly injured and bleeding into my abdominal cavity. The agony I felt was indescribable.

After regaining consciousness, I looked up. I was lying under a massive oak tree with a rope swing. As I tried to process what was happening, I heard my kids crying out in pain. When I realized they had been bucked off the horse, I tried to get up and couldn't move. Immediately, the Lord blessed me with an inner assurance that they were okay. I knew Alex was attending to them.

When I started to get my bearings, I managed to prop myself up slightly onto one elbow and look around. I remember thinking, *I'm going to die.* Pleading with God to spare my life, I begged Him not take me. My children were my whole world. I wanted to watch them grow up, get married, and have families of their own.

The pain was unbearable. In agony, I wondered, *why isn't anyone checking on me?* Unbelievably, no one saw what happened.

My friend, Elizabeth, finally came over to me and knelt down. She asked me if I had fallen off the rope swing. I motioned *no.* She said, "You'll be okay, you've just had the wind knocked out of you." Her words were comforting to me.

Troy came running over. He said to his wife, Elizabeth, "I think she got kicked by the horse." I kept trying to shake my head *yes.*

As soon as people started realizing what happened, everyone was in a state of shock. Somehow I managed to say the word *blessing*, and had to repeat it over and over. More than anything I desired to have a priesthood blessing. Finally, they understood. Troy put his hands on my head and blessed me that my internal organs would calm down. Immediately, I felt everything relax. I was able to breathe better.

Elizabeth kept asking, "Would you like me to call an ambulance?" I nodded, "Yes."

Instantly, I wondered if I would live until the ambulance showed up.

The paramedics arrived and asked me where I was hurting. I pointed to my liver which was filling up with blood. Immediately, they ripped off my clothes, leapt into action, and started poking me with needles. The EMTs wanted to life flight me but didn't think they could find a landing spot for the helicopter. They decided to transport me by ambulance and used Velcro straps to secure me to the stretcher.

Upon arrival at the hospital they gave me morphine. The doctor said I would be prepped for surgery. If the internal bleeding didn't stop they would have to cut me open, pull my liver out of my body, and pack it with foam and ice. The surgery was life-threatening.

In intensive care, they prepped me for the procedure. I had lost so much blood that I needed a transfusion. During the transfusion, many family members came in to see me. When I saw my brother-in-law, Mitch, I asked him to anoint my head with oil and give me another priesthood blessing. In the name of Jesus Christ, he pronounced a beautiful blessing upon me. Right away my condition improved. Incredibly, the bleeding slowed down and finally stopped. The doctor was amazed. There was no scientific explanation for what happened. Shaking his head, he announced that I didn't have to have surgery. It was a miracle.

I was so limp, pale, and weak, it took all of the energy I had to will myself to live. I was in the hospital for ten days. When I was released, I could barely get up and walk around. It was impossible for me to care for myself or my children. Even though Alex and I were still separated, out of necessity, he would spend the nights at the house to help me and the kids. He stayed with us for five months. This was a grueling time for me as I wondered what the future held for our family. I hoped that this experience would bring Alex and me together, reminding him of how precious our family and marriage was.

When I was physically stable, Alex moved out.

My heart was broken. Day after day, I would sit in my recliner with my kids surrounding me, doing my best to help us all survive. With a long road of physical and emotional healing ahead, I was alone caring for my kids. My two oldest children were ages 7 and 9, so they helped a lot with the younger ones. It took me a year to fully recover.

Just as life was getting to a tolerable place, my mother passed away. This was another grueling time for our family. My youngest sister was thirteen-years-old and, without warning, I was given permanent custody of her. I was still separated from my husband and was now responsible for five children. In order for us to survive, I had to seek employment out of the home.

In spite of Heavenly Father's watchful care, my husband's addiction led him to other destructive behaviors, and he went down a path that led to criminal activity.

There are things worse than divorce.

After doing everything within my power to save our marriage, divorce proceedings were under way. As a child, I promised myself that I would never get divorced. Breaking that promise made my heart reel. I was not only fighting for my own survival but for the survival of my children. The Lord has always been there for me, yet the trials I've been given have felt overwhelming.

Shortly after our divorce finalized, I experienced one of the most difficult tests of my faith. One evening, I walked outside and my van was gone—disappeared. My only means of transporting five children under the age of 14 was stolen right out from under me while I sat inside my house.

A few weeks earlier, I'd lost my job. The means of security I had to support my family dissolved. Now, with no van, my children and I were both physically and financially stranded. After exhausting all efforts to work with the police, I had to accept that my van was gone. I'd been at the end of my rope several times in my life before and had faced many excruciating trials, yet each time I knew that God wouldn't give me more than I could handle.

This time was different. I became unglued.

Fortunately, I have been blessed with friends, ward members, and loved ones who have been a support to me. My friend, Josie, had also been through a brutal divorce. She had been praying for me and felt impressed to tell her brother, Tom, and sister-in-law, Amy, about my situation. Many of Josie's extended family members were also praying for our family.

One evening, after getting the children settled in for the night, I couldn't sleep. The weight of my responsibilities came crashing down around me. It felt like my life was spinning out of control and I was not in the driver's seat. I went to the kitchen but I wasn't hungry, so I did what I always did—I began pleading with God for help. Sorrow and grief overwhelmed me, and I literally dropped to my knees on the floor. I poured my heart out to my Father in Heaven.

I felt like I could take no more; I had been wrung out in every possible way.

As I continued my supplication, I was very specific—I said that I needed a vehicle that was already paid for because I didn't have enough money for a car payment. I wanted a more reliable car than the stolen van. Somehow, I thought, that would help make up for the great loss I was suffering. Although our prayers are not always answered in the way we want, I have found that the more detailed the prayer, the more specific the blessing. As I prayed, I was open to God's will and was honest, clear, and specific about my desires.

I kept praying until I was ready to drop. Exhausted, I finally forced myself to move, and stumbled into my bedroom. It took every last ounce of energy I had to pry myself out of bed the next morning. It was as though I was on autopilot, although for some reason, I felt an increased measure of peace.

Later that day, I received a message from a business asking me to call back. I recognized the company; my friend Josie had a brother who was the owner. Josie knew of my desperate need for work, and I hoped she had talked to her brother, Tom, for me. I was excited—what if the call was about an interview for a job?

Tom called me back. In a matter-of-fact tone, he told me that he and his family were going to give me their van. It took a minute to register. I felt as though I might pass out. *Did I understand him correctly? Did he just say he was going to give me his van? What would he drive? How could I possibly accept such a tremendous gift? And yet, isn't this exactly what I had just prayed for?*

Methodically, I hung up the phone. A multitude of mixed feelings hit me all at once—intense gratitude, relief, and embarrassment. I wondered how to thank someone for giving me a van. Words hardly seemed adequate. His offering was overwhelming and I didn't know how to respond. We set up a time for him and his family to come over that afternoon. I spent the next few hours trying to make my mind believe that someone I barely knew was giving me their van.

When this beautiful family showed up at my home, I was touched. They seemed like an army of angels. The humility of Tom, his wife, Amy, and their children, had a powerful impact on me and my kids. Amy's caring eyes were wet with emotion. I was very much affected by her lovely countenance that exuded love. The adults and many of the children were in tears. I'll never forget that day for as long as I live; it's permanently etched on my heart, my memory, and my very being, forever.

As I accepted the van, I felt giddy, happy, light, yet very insecure. I was overcome with a swirling mixture of opposing emotions—relief at having our needs met and my prayers answered in such an amazing way. Simultaneously, I felt intimidation mixed with embarrassment and pain for my destitute circumstances. Guilt consumed me because I felt so undeserving. I didn't know what to say—I was in shock. My kids had the same reaction.

I had little to offer in return except gratitude. My simple note of thanks was handwritten on a plain piece of paper. When I think about the experience, I get choked up—it was so sacred. Every time we enter that vehicle, we feel thankfulness for that family's kindness and generosity. I'm reminded of how much I am loved by our Father in Heaven.

Praying every day for basic needs has been a normal way of life for me and for my children. I needed a van that would run, and I was given one in mint condition, far beyond what could have gotten us by. I've had to learn that I deserve things I want; not just the things I need. The Lord is helping me grasp that lesson.

We are a critical link in each other's lives. Josie cared about my situation. She knew about the stolen van and our other destitute circumstances, and she suffered right along with me. Josie passed on her love and concern to Amy and Tom, who, in turn, gave me a vehicle, but ultimately they gave me hope.

The circle of giving and receiving is an endless circle. I like to think of it as one continuous round. I went from having no vehicle to having one I can share. And you know what? There have been times when a friend in need, another single mom, has needed a vehicle. The circle has come back around.

At times, we may not feel like we have much to give, yet now I'm married to the most wonderful and faithful man who is truly my best friend. He is honest, caring, righteous, and incredibly trustworthy. Our wedding rings remind me of the circle of service, one continuous round. Together, we hope to someday be in a position where we can follow the example of Tom and Amy—give away a vehicle to someone in need. For now, we are happy to share.

Mile Marker Five: Be a Driving Force in God's Miracles

Before Bailey was compensated with a van in mint condition, her faith was tested in unthinkable ways. As her friend, it was hard to accept the unfair trials in Bailey's life. But the Lord was in control, preparing to compensate her. He united these faithful friends together as a driving force in His miracles. When trials aren't fair, I ask myself the following two questions:

Question 1: Am I experiencing this trial because I sinned?

If a trial is because of our own sins, and we want to feel relief from the guilt and pain, we need to sincerely repent. Repentance means good news—a change of heart. Through the atoning blood of Christ, we can be clean. Sincere repentance will not change the natural consequences of our choices, and this can be a bitter pill to swallow. Through the enabling power of Jesus Christ's Atonement, we will be strengthened to endure and accept our present circumstances.

Question 2: Am I experiencing this trial because of my inexperience, an error in judgment, human weakness, or another's agency?

If a trial is not the result of our own sins, the Lord is allowing us to be molded spiritually. Heavenly Father usually doesn't interfere with the agency of others; agency is an eternal law. Our experiences may have been propelled by our lack of judgment, humanness, or the free will of another, but the Lord is not punishing us. He is stretching us beyond our own spiritual capacity.

Elder Joseph B. Wirthlin reminds us of the compensating nature of Jesus Christ:

"The Lord compensates the faithful for *every* loss. That which is taken away from those who love the Lord will be added unto them in His own way. While it may not come at the time we desire, the faithful will know that every tear today will eventually be returned a *hundredfold* with tears of rejoicing and gratitude." (Joseph B. Wirthlin, "Come What May, and Love It," *Ensign*, Nov 2008, p. 28, emphasis added)

My experiences with Bailey taught me to:

- *Pray in faith for specific ways to be a driving force in God's miracles.*

- *Determine if a trial is because of humanness or sin, and then repent if needed.*

- *Acknowledge the compensating nature of the Lord.*

- *Have the vision to see and accept others who are prompted by God to serve us through the trials of divorce.*

Questions

What are some trials you have faced during your divorce or the divorce of someone close to you? Were they caused by human weakness or sin? Where are you at emotionally in reconciling these trials with yourself and the Lord?

_____
_____
_____
_____
_____
_____

How have others shown you mercy and love during divorce-related experiences? Were you able to accept their gifts? How can you pay it forward?

_____
_____
_____
_____
_____
_____

How has God compensated you for losses stemming from divorce? Have you thanked Him? Write Heavenly Father a thank you note showing gratitude for the blessings you have received.

_____
_____
_____
_____
_____
_____

Chapter Six

Shifting Gears: Kate's Homosexual Husband

Kate and I have been friends since childhood. I have many fond memories of sleepovers when we were naive, giggly girls, back when we truly believed that we would find our handsome princes and live happily ever after—the first time. Kate looked like a Disney princess to me with her small frame and blond hair. As we grew up, we confided in each other our grand hopes and dreams for the future. We never imagined we would both get divorced; it was unthinkable. When I heard of Kate's divorce, I was stunned. My life had become so heavy with heartache that I hadn't been able to be there for support when she found out that her husband was gay.

Kate's story in her own words

In the early 1990s, very few members of the Church conversed openly about homosexuality beyond our fears of the AIDS epidemic, which was hitting the United States. Not once, before I married Lance, did he confide in me his struggles with homosexuality. After he came out, someone once asked me, "Did he think getting married would shift him?" I have often wondered this myself.

Ours is a tragic love story of letting go.

Lance and I met at a leadership conference during our senior year of high school. He was amusing and genuinely attractive. He was student body president and earned a very prestigious scholarship. He was ambitious and driven—as a fledgling musician and composer, he was constantly playing, sketching or writing. Initially, I wasn't interested in Lance, but over time, our friendship blossomed and I became enamored with his musical talents and spiritual gifts.

For a time, Lance read the entire *Book of Mormon* every month. Good grief, we were in high school! Where did this drive come from? He was obsessed with scriptures about light and often talked about his belief that we could all be conduits of the light of God. Before graduation, he wrote on the wallet-size senior picture he gave me, "Kate, go toward the light, which is so abundant once you find the source."

After graduation, we both began college and then left to serve missions. We faithfully wrote to each other, and Lance proposed while I was still serving. He returned home six months before me. I came home from my mission engaged to Lance, ready to start this new chapter in my life. We had never actually dated, so our two-and-a-half month engagement was also our courtship. I assumed that our deep friendship and shared spirituality were a recipe for success.

Being physical with Lance felt foreign. He and I had never been romantic, and suddenly I was kissing my fiancé and planning our wedding. Our kissing felt very bland and a bit too chaste, but I assumed it was because I was still adjusting to post-mission life. I was very attracted to Lance, but looking back, I mistook the excitement of our whirlwind romance as chemistry. We were *never* tempted to take things too far. I have since learned that when two people have sexual chemistry, they should both be tempted to *not* be chaste—or something is very wrong.

We married in the temple, but from the beginning something felt wrong in our relationship. Our physical intimacy seemed dark. Although the men I had dated in the past made me feel desirable, Lance didn't seem attracted to me at all. I began to feel very insecure.

Two months after our wedding, I had a dream about Lance. In it, he was wearing a satin robe adorned with peacocks, and he flounced around showing off his home décor to his friends. Without telling Lance about the dream, I began to carefully observe him and started to notice some stereotypical homosexual tendencies. I would pick up on a clue and then convince myself to dismiss it. He liked decorating our home an awful lot. So what? A lot of men do. He loved theater and often purchased Broadway CDs. Sure, but all kinds of people like musicals, right? I was totally in denial. Unfortunately, before we got married, it never occurred to me that I might want to ask him if he had same-sex feelings of attraction.

Six months after we were married, Lance wanted to audition for a summer theatre company. It was not lucrative, and we were trying to stay afloat without student loans. I felt that with our financial concerns, this was not a responsible thing to do but he auditioned anyway. He landed the job and insisted on taking it, leaving him to spend most of his free time with the male cast members—all of whom turned out to be gay. One of the women in the cast sought me out in order to warn me of a homosexual incident regarding Lance and another cast member.

I was stunned beyond description. *Could this really be true? Is my husband actually gay?* The questions were shocking. We went on a drive and I tearfully confronted Lance. He confessed and seemed truly sorry. He immediately made attempts to repent, which resulted in church disciplinary action. His efforts allowed me to feel a glimmer of hope amidst my heartbreak, but I was still in complete shock. Worried that it was me, I had a total image makeover from head to toe. To my distress, nothing changed in the way he responded toward me.

Only a few months later, I learned he was having an affair.

Angrily, I asked him why he kept hurting me, and if he really wanted to be married to me. Then, I fled our apartment to spend some time with the only two friends he had agreed I could tell. I felt so much insecurity that I became paranoid, questioning him every time he came home late. We both felt so isolated and alone, neither of us knowing what to do next.

Lance would not mention divorce, and I wasn't ready to take the initiative myself. I was absolutely sure that I wanted to remain true to my marriage covenants. The agony of losing my husband was too life-shattering. I researched others with this struggle who had stayed married. How had they done it? Could he really change if he wanted to? Swearing each other to secrecy, we carried on. If Lance would promise to not act on his homosexuality, I could accept that he was not physically attracted to me. We still loved each other and planned to suffer in silence.

I still remember the time I had to leave our apartment during a bridal shower I was hosting because I had become overwhelmed by my feelings of sadness and impending doom. The bride-to-be was full of hopes and dreams; I was having a panic attack.

Lance and I decided we needed a new start. We had both landed jobs working for the United Nations in Geneva, Switzerland, so we got summer jobs in the Grand Canyon North Rim Lodge to save enough money to move abroad in the fall.

One morning, I opened a credit card bill that had just arrived and saw that Lance had purchased expensive gifts for his male lover. The betrayal stung even more as I realized he had spent more money on this man than on any gift he had ever given me.

I confronted Lance, who admitted he was still having an affair. We argued late into the night to the point of exhaustion. My scornful accusations reflected my outrage. Was I of any value to him at all? Facing reality meant that perhaps he could not reciprocate my feelings of marital and sexual love. Lance cared more about his lover's feelings than mine. He gave me no reassurance, appearing completely numb and despondent. Unable to reach a resolution, we finally fell asleep.

Early the next morning, I awoke feeling burdened and restless. I wrote a poem while laying on a lawn chair on the roof of the lodge. I needed to record the evidence of my hurt. After pouring the feelings of my heart onto paper, and feeling utterly alone, I went outside for a run. As I ran alongside the road parallel to the edge of the Grand Canyon, I watched as the morning sunlight and clouds made patterns of light and darkness around me. Never, in my entire life, had I felt so completely hopeless. I considered committing suicide by jumping off the canyon rim.

A cautionary shock went through me as I realized that no one would stop me if I jumped.

What had happened to me? I felt like a stranger in my own life. Dangerous thoughts were racing around in my head, but I could find no answers. The burden was too much for me to handle alone and I was being destroyed from the inside out. Desperately needing help, I pleaded with the Lord for some relief from my paralyzing loneliness and heartache.

What more could I do? I had done everything I could think of and had done my best to educate myself about Lance's struggles. Thinking I might be the problem, I had even tried to completely change myself in order to make myself more attractive to him, but nothing had worked. I needed more divine assurance to continue in the direction I was going; I needed a friend. But who could I talk to? We had chosen to tell only a few trusted people about our situation, and neither of our families knew anything about our anguish.

My Heavenly Father, who knew about all of my unspoken needs, lovingly intervened. A few hours later, after my near suicide, my older brother called out of the blue. He is a pilot and the next day he had a twenty-four hour layover in St. George, Utah. He asked if I would like to join him. We decided to meet at the temple. The timing was such a tender mercy.

While at the temple, I fasted for the courage to tell him what was happening in my life. I felt a prompting to talk to a woman who was sitting near me, following the session, but I fought the impression. I was too hurt and had no emotional energy. What would I say to her anyway? "Hi, my husband, who I love more than anyone else in the world, is gay. Should I divorce him?"

When I returned to the sisters' dressing room, the same woman was at the end of the aisle. As I approached her, our eyes met and she said quietly, "The Lord asked me to talk to you. Do you have a minute?" Unbelievably, she had faced a similar experience to mine. She explained how a woman's mental, physical, and spiritual health has limits. She had nearly destroyed herself, spending years trying to maintain a very damaging marriage by carrying a weight far too great. When she finally divorced, irreparable harm had been done. She felt it would take the rest of her life to recover. She counseled me, "I know you will find your own way, but please do not do what I have done." I knew God had sent her to me.

I confided in my brother over dinner; he listened with love and a desire to protect me. He encouraged me to seek a trial separation from my husband. While he did not suggest a divorce, sharing the burden with him provided enough relief for me to begin an emotional separation.

The next day, I returned to the Grand Canyon's North Rim, girded with strength. Deep down, I knew I needed to leave. That night, as I laid in bed beside Lance, I realized that this might be the last time I would be allowed to gaze upon his body and face in this way. This was the only man with whom I had shared my entire self. He was asleep, so I began to say goodbye as I wept over each feature I had come to adore. The experience felt solemn and sacred. It was easier while he was unaware. As I said goodbye to his body, my own body seemed to withdraw into itself entirely, and I felt as if I was going into a cocoon.

The next week, while at work, I struck up a conversation with a nice couple in the dining room. For some reason, I told them about my dilemma with my homosexual husband. When I came back with their food, in great sobriety, the gentleman cautioned me, "Look, if you were my daughter, I would take you home this instant. This is not something to trifle with—get out. You are risking your life and your health. If he is not being faithful, *you could get AIDS!*"

His words gave me the courage I needed to finally meet my own needs. I packed up a few belongings and then told Lance I was going to see my parents for a long weekend. He begged me to stay and give him more time to sort things out, but I bluntly refused. I could see more clearly now. Lance was stalling—making feeble attempts to cover things up. He did not want me to tell his family. Ever. The secrecy was killing me.

I loaded my suitcase and began to drive. My internal struggle began again—I was still in denial. *It would be so much easier if we finished our summer jobs and ran away to Switzerland! Why not try? This didn't have to determine our lives!* In my haze of thought, I didn't realize I was speeding and an officer pulled me over. I blurted out that I was driving home to tell my parents about my gay husband. With a troubled face, he bade me farewell and wished me luck.

Then I began to pray aloud—this was going to be a long seven hours. I begged God to help me not turn around. I suddenly saw two hitchhikers on the side of the highway. I felt prompted to do the unthinkable: I picked them up. Desperate for the company, I practiced telling these young men what I would say to my parents, and they listened. Later, I dropped them off and said goodbye, grateful for their presence.

When I arrived at my parent's home, they were expecting a big announcement. Was I pregnant? Was someone seriously ill? Somehow, I found the courage to tell them. The news visibly upset them, but their profound love and concern helped me along. They promised to keep my confidence, while we made plans for my new future. A few days later, we drove back to the Grand Canyon, gathered the remainder of my things, left the car to my husband, and drove home.

Numbness enveloped me. For a while, I lived with my parents. I needed to belong somewhere, and their comforting words of reassurance truly held me together at times. I felt so fragile and absolutely stunned by the hurt from my husband who had promised to love and cherish me. I wondered if my depressed state would ever end. Was I doomed to feel this way for the rest of my life? Would I ever be able to stop loving someone who could not love me back?

During our separation, rehashing my dramatic story to those closest to me, and feeling pressure to tell everyone what had happened, was grueling. Realizing that the demise of my marriage was a result of my husband being gay left many people at a complete loss for words.

I needed professional counseling since, deep down, I was still in love with Lance. After I left the Grand Canyon, he had gone to a clinic for gay men in the Church who wanted to re-frame themselves. He really tried, but to no avail. I realized that I needed to stop focusing on a way to reorient my husband for a marriage that no longer existed. I had been obsessing about what was going to happen to him. Through therapy, I learned that I needed to stop living in the past. But I still deeply cared about Lance, and sometimes I could not help myself.

My therapist encouraged me to find ways to relax and have fun. This coping mechanism proved to distract me from my heartache for a little while, but my mind and heart always went back to my near-constant state of sadness. I saw a medical doctor and asked about anti-depressant medication. This was an option and he was willing to prescribe something. He also suggested regular exercise as a way of raising my endorphins. I didn't really want to start taking anti-depressants, so I determined to set up a rigorous exercise schedule and stick to it five days a week. What a world of difference this made for me.

The next week a friend encouraged me to schedule testing for sexually transmitted diseases. I dreaded this, but knew she was right. Because of my husband's immoral actions, I had contracted chlamydia! It was a disease which is easily treatable, but if left untreated, can cause sterility. I was both shocked and thankful. Had I waited, it may have been too late.

The day I was to sign the divorce papers, Lance called me from San Francisco. He was very ill and in the hospital. He described having a dream of himself in old age, dying alone. He wanted to try again and asked me to please wait. He wanted to move to the area where I lived.

I postponed signing the papers, but told him that the only way I would consider this was if he lived on his own and proved to me by his actions that he truly wanted to reconcile. My feelings were all over the place. I was a mess but decided to help him secure an apartment.

Shortly after, I made an appointment with Elder F. Enzio Busche, the regional representative over our area. In his office, he gave Lance a blessing which spoke about the noble spirit he was in the pre-existence, and the weight and urgency of his decisions. He was told he could choose to stop his affairs and stay faithful to his covenants if he wanted to stay married.

We thanked Elder Busche for the blessing. When I asked Lance about the blessing, he said he hadn't felt the Spirit for so long that he had only basked in the feeling and had no idea what was said. Astounded, I typed up what I could remember and gave it to him. That was the last thing I ever gave him—a transcription of that blessing, hoping it would make a difference.

Lance lived near me for the next three months. He was lost, constantly asking me for money and frequently in and out of jobs. At times he showed some interest in me, but mostly I pursued him. I would stop by after work and ask him how things were going, but our times together were strained and uncomfortable. During one of my visits, I saw a metro area gay newspaper in his apartment.

That was the last straw.

I called Elder Busche and described my husband's lack of any measurable effort to salvage our marriage. His response was unequivocal: "There comes a time when we must move forward. You have a divine role and must help in building the kingdom of God." These words left an indelible impression upon me. Finally, I was ready to divorce Lance.

Two years after our wedding, we signed divorce papers. At the attorney's office, we asked for a few moments together. I hadn't seen Lance in months, but I still cared deeply for him and my heart hurt all over again because of the broken dreams we could not fix. We held each other close as we wept, knowing the end was in sight; this was merely a shell of a marriage.

Needing a change of scenery, I left the country for a four month position in Basel, Switzerland. My former boss, who had hired me for an internship during my separation and divorce, hired me as a nanny. This was a wonderful grace period, where I filled my love supply with the authentic love shown me from the children I cared for. I reciprocated this love, which helped fill my empty heart. I also reconnected with my extended family roots.

When I returned to the United States, I needed direction. I decided to attend the university where I had lived with my ex-husband. My dating and social life felt much different at age 24, with some raw and painful life experiences as a frame of reference. I enjoyed single dating, sharing who I was and what I'd been through. Twice after my divorce, I began to date someone exclusively, only to realize I was still not ready. I was still grieving Lance.

During this time I had a spiritual moment in the Salt Lake Temple. For an instant, I sensed the presence of my future children surrounding me as if in a circle of love and comfort. I remember saying in my heart, "I feel you here, I really do, but I don't even know who your father is!" After that experience, I prayed more fervently that the Lord would help me find him. I could feel my hope and desire for a future family of my own getting stronger.

Heavenly Father answered my request and, knowing my desires, a temple marriage was on its way. At school, I met a man named Gabe who did not blink twice when I told him my story.

Experiences in Gabe's life had prepared him for me and he was a great comfort to me. Gabe let me ask him all kinds of "what if" questions to test him. His answers demonstrated the kind of straightforward companionship I needed to soothe my soul; soon we were inseparable. Gabe asked me if he could be the one to heal the parts of my heart that had been scarred.

On the day of our wedding, Gabe and I were both emotional. My tears stemmed from the knowledge of God's guiding hand, placing us in each other's lives. In my marriage to Gabe I could sense his devotion. I was slowly learning to develop trust in our partnership. When he would come home a few minutes late, I would fall apart. Patiently, he would reassure me. I knew this marriage was different from the last one. No matter what, Gabe was always kind to me.

Within our first few years of marriage, we moved far away to continue our studies. That experience taught us to rely on each other and the Lord for our support. We have been married for twenty-five years now, through poverty and plenty, through graduate school and careers. Both of us strive to be loyal, fun, honest, and true to our covenants. We never run out of things to say or places to explore. Together we have created a beautiful family.

My ex-husband still found his way to Europe. He married a man and moved on with his life. While he is no longer active in the Church, he has good relationships with his family.

I have not yet solved the mystery of how homosexuality fits into God's plan after this life, but I do know for sure that we are accountable for our actions toward one another, particularly during a marriage. I don't believe Lance understood all of the implications of marrying a woman. He was simply trying to do what was right. A priesthood blessing told me that God would call upon me one day to stand as a witness both for and against my ex-husband.

The day of reckoning will come for all of us, and our loving Savior, Jesus Christ, will be our eternal judge. Until then, it is up to us to strive to do our best and to make good decisions. There are successful marriages where partners have gay tendencies. The key is honesty and humility. Ultimately, marital success comes down to the proper use of agency by both partners.

We all have lessons to learn. Sometimes the knowledge we gain in this life is hard-earned through very difficult experiences. Fully realizing the implications of Lance's homosexuality turned my dreams for a beautiful marriage into the ashes of divorce. Over time, I have come to appreciate that it was the light between the shadows of my experience which created the shapes that eventually outlined my future path. My great suffering both strengthened and refined my faith. But at the time of our divorce, oh my goodness, there was unbelievable heartache.

Mile Marker Six: Keep Your Eyes Wide Open

After collecting divorce stories for this book for many years, it finally felt complete. Then one morning while on a walk, I started thinking about Kate's divorce. Suddenly, I knew her story needed to be included. Kate was a busy mother caring for five children. Would she want to share it? Or have time? I had deadlines—what was God thinking? Oh wait, God's timing is perfect.

I called Kate and asked if she would like to share her experiences. To my surprise, she told me about a blessing she had received during her divorce. In the blessing, she was told to write down her experiences and to share them with the world.

Kate's story reminds me that unhealthy secrets affect self-esteem and can lead to self-loathing, self-harm, or suicide.

Just as Jesus Christ was both strong and compassionate, we

really need measures of both love and boundaries to have safe and thriving relationships. Resentment kills marriages, and both men and women need to come forward and deal with things as soon as they flare-up. If not, misunderstandings and mistakes too often become a cancer that at some point is irreversible.

If clear and assertive boundaries are established early in a marriage, and vigorously defended in a loving way with a lot of feedback, so many of these challenging situations could be resolved instead of marriages torn apart before Dr. Laura's "Three A's" (Adultery, Addiction, or Abuse) take hold as a result of hardened hearts.

Remember, we can only set boundaries for ourselves. For example, telling a spouse that they can't yell at you is trying to control your partner. Instead, setting a healthy boundary would be telling your spouse what you will do *if* they choose to yell at you. Understanding healthy boundaries deserves time and attention, especially after a divorce.

I know couples who have faced adultery, addiction, and abuse head on, and their marriages have evolved into healthy marriages. When *both partners* have addressed these issues with humility and a desire to change, through the enabling power of the Atonement of Jesus Christ, miracles can happen.

My journey with Kate reminded me that:

- *Full disclosure of one's past is critical before marriage.*
- *Heavenly Father will help us find the courage to end unsafe relationships.*
- *Understanding and setting boundaries for ourselves is critical for a healthy marriage.*
- *We should not attempt to control our partner or anyone in the name of "setting a boundary."*

Questions

Sometimes God allows us to be deceived to try our faith. If you are married, or divorced, were you deceived prior to marriage? Did you deceive your spouse? If so, how did the deceit affect the trust in your marriage?

_____
_____
_____
_____
_____

Are there any relationships you might need to distance yourself from to preserve your emotional and spiritual safety?

_____
_____
_____
_____
_____

Describe your beliefs about healthy boundaries. If you have divorced, in your prior marriage, did you set healthy boundaries for yourself? Did you ever attempt to control your spouse in the "name" of setting a boundary?

_____
_____
_____
_____
_____

Chapter Seven

Blindsided by Agency: The Treks of Two Good Men

One summer, I attended a church service in Park City, Utah. I was riveted by the spiritual depth of the sacrament meeting speaker and felt this man had been through significant life experiences. I was struggling to understand the principle of agency and his talk was enlightening. After the meeting, I introduced myself and learned that Tim had survived several divorces. He was willing to share his story with me. Simultaneously, I was rekindling a friendship with Luke, a longtime friend who was blindsided by a second divorce. Both of these handsome and impressive men seemed totally sincere. As they struggled to accept the agency of their wives, writing their stories for this chapter helped me further understand choice and accountability.

Tim's Story in His Own Words

After several divorces, I wondered if I would ever find a lifelong companion. In spite of incredible opposition, I believed I would find a wife. I kept looking and still had high hopes for an eternal marriage.

Three years after my second divorce, I met Donna, a new convert to the Church. She seemed solid in the Gospel and we connected right away. She was beautiful and had a great personality. Within a few weeks, our dating had become serious. Donna was an accomplished woman and I was impressed that she had developed many talents and written a book.

We dated for three months and then married. When we returned from our honeymoon, we visited Donna's parents on the way home. They were great people, very warm and friendly. I felt accepted by them as well as her extended family members. I was hopeful that the third time would be the charm—I had found my soul mate.

Shortly after the wedding, I started noticing some weird behaviors from Donna. She began making claims that didn't seem true. She would never show me the book she insisted that she had written and published. In detail, she would describe the writing process, the research, and how she had worked hard to accomplish such a lofty goal, but never produced the book. When I questioned her, she would talk in circles—telling me lavish detailed stories, giving me reasons that didn't make sense. It was like talking to a politician.

Donna told me her parents had inherited a large sum of money, but the inheritance was never discussed by other extended family members. Things weren't adding up in many areas of her life and she offered no proof to substantiate her claims. It made me anxious and I began to wonder about her integrity.

Two months into our marriage, I received the most shocking phone call of my life. I answered the phone and heard an unfamiliar voice on the other end.

"Hi, Tim. This is Robert."

"Robert who?"

"Robert Simmons. Donna's ex-husband."

My heart started racing. Donna had told me many stories about the legendary Robert. I was grateful Donna had the courage to walk away from such an abusive man.

"Donna is at a hair appointment. Can I help you?"

"If you would be willing to talk with me, I would really appreciate it."

I wasn't thrilled about talking with Robert. Donna had painted him out to be a horrible man. She had described how he had caused her significant emotional pain throughout the years of their marriage.

As the conversation progressed, a bomb dropped.

"I have been trying to find Donna for several years now. During our marriage she started lying to me about different things—a lot. Our marriage was rocky from the beginning. Suddenly, she left in a rage and had her phone number changed, making it virtually impossible to track her down. She left me without any contact information. A series of events led me to you. Finding your phone number was a miracle."

The anxiety in his voice felt strangely familiar.

"The reason I'm calling is I am still legally married to Donna."

Wrapping my mind around this news seemed impossible. I was blown away.

"Finally, I can divorce Donna. It's been horrible being married on paper for years without having a way to end it legally. When I learned she had remarried, I was shocked."

Robert advised me to call Donna's parents. I did, and they were alarmed with the news. They had no idea she had not divorced Robert. Donna had painted an in-depth picture of her messy divorce, the cost involved, and how horrible Robert had been. Now Donna's parents were reeling as well.

While Donna was at her hair appointment, I took the opportunity to make as many phone calls as possible. Further research verified that she hadn't divorced Stan, the husband before Robert. Donna was married to *three* men.

When Donna came home from the salon, she was cold and robotic. Obviously, before her arrival, she'd talked with her parents and been caught in her lies. I tried to talk with her and make sense of what was happening. She was distant and all she said was that she hadn't divorced Stan or Robert because she "didn't like paperwork."

Without warning, my life had become a soap opera. I quickly consulted an attorney and learned that our marriage could be annulled. Donna said she was leaving me for good and needed a ride to the airport that evening. We drove in icy silence. Dropping her off at the terminal was the last time I ever saw her.

My life felt out of control and I was completely devastated. I faced a test that involved the principles of choice and accountability. How could this happen?

Before Donna left, I could have argued with her or tried to reason with her to make her stay. Ultimately, I didn't want to control Donna, or use guilt to convince her into staying with me and changing her life. Deep down, I knew that if I hampered her agency, neither of us would have the opportunity to learn from our experiences; but I loved my wife. This challenge tested my patience in unique and unexpected ways. I was tempted to head down a dark path and learned many tough lessons along the way.

I learned that when we veer off the Lord's path, there is always hope. Regardless of how lost we are, with God's help we can plot a course to regain our footing. As we study the Gospel of Jesus Christ, the Spirit will guide us through the uncharted territory of divorce.

The scriptures are like road signs given to us by the Lord, guiding us on earth while our spirits are under construction. A living prophet and apostles are like the construction workers on the road, ever pointing, directing, and beckoning us toward safe paths. When we don't pay attention to the Lord's construction crew and follow His signs, we will eventually get lost.

For a time I was totally lost. I had the opportunity to grow spiritually by accepting Donna's agency. But I didn't want to grow. I wanted my wife. My grueling test was accepting that I needed to exercise *my* agency and let Donna go. As I stayed on the Lord's path through study, prayer, and following the prophet, eventually I gained the spiritual strength to let go.

Luke's Story in His Own Words

After many long and lonely years of being single after a first divorce, and trying to find my eternal companion, I finally met and married the love of my life. I could not believe the Lord had remembered me and blessed me so much to marry Jennifer. Over and over, I told myself I loved her as much as any man has ever loved a wife. But to my great dismay, she left me several times during the first few months of our marriage, threatening divorce.

Each time Jennifer left, she came back, until she finally left, never to return. To make the situation worse, she was pregnant when she left for good. The pain was so tremendous that I truly never imagined the human soul could endure such exquisite agony.

One way of describing the pain is to quote from the journal of my good friend's pioneer ancestor. This great woman was part of the Willie Handcart Company. In her journal she writes:

"In the month of June, 1857, my husband went on a mission to England, and after I had worked for upwards of four years to maintain myself and little one, my husband himself sent word that he never intended to set foot in Utah again. And here I must be allowed to say on behalf of myself and other true women who have endured such separations, and to whom, perhaps, it is counted as nothing; no one can realize what such an ordeal is unless they have passed through it. All that I had hitherto suffered seemed like *child's play* compared to being deserted by the one in whom I had chosen to place the utmost confidence, who himself had fixed an impassable gulf between us by ignoring the very principles by which he had obtained me, leaving myself and my little one (for all he knew) to sorrow and destitution." (emphasis added)

It is quite overwhelming to realize that this pioneer woman who had suffered so much in leaving her family in England, and in her journey crossing the plains, still said of her husband leaving her, "All that I had hitherto suffered seemed like *child's play* compared to being deserted by the one in whom I had chosen to place the utmost confidence."

All I can similarly say is that no pain I have ever endured in this life comes remotely close to the profound suffering and sorrow I felt when my wife left me. Words cannot describe the pain, the tears, the heart-wrenching agony I suffered over her for so many months, and there is still sadness when I think back on it.

Each time Jennifer left, my pain and sorrow was renewed. I was left to wonder if I could survive another minute before dying. Hour after hour, day after day, and month after month, I had no choice but to endure. I could not understand why my wife continued to leave me. She wouldn't communicate with me and explain what was wrong.

I survived that time because of the mercy of the Lord and the many blessings my Heavenly Father gave me. He made sure that the hundreds of hours of prayers, fasting, and support from my family, the help of my bishop, and the encouragement of friends were there to help me make it through.

Depression overcame me. I had to seek medical help and leave my job for several weeks—neither of which had I ever done before.

I constantly prayed and read from the *Doctrine and Covenants*, Sections 121 and 122, when Joseph Smith was in the Liberty Jail and prayed to God for mercy saying, "O God, where art thou and where is the pavilion that covereth thy hiding place?" (D&C 121:1) I constantly thought of the suffering that our Savior went through and I knew that only He understood my pain.

Many family members and friends supported me and helped carry my burdens. One particularly sweet person, who worked for me, told me that one night the Lord revealed to him that he needed to look after me until I was alright. He said it was perhaps the greatest spiritual experience of his life when the Spirit told him to watch over his boss. He called me, stopped by, left notes on my door, and kept a constant watch over me.

Friends that I hadn't seen much suddenly had impressions to call me, pray for me, or come by to see me. The miracle of charity and kindness from friends, family, and mostly from my loving parents who had just returned from a long, arduous mission, was indescribable.

My wife had our baby a few months after she left. Not being at his birth was another tremendous blow to my already fragile state. My emotional pain became physically manifested. I felt as though I had lost a close family member, such as my mother or father, with no explanation, and would not be with them for the rest of my life or eternity.

In the end, my bishop told me that I'd done nothing wrong, that I was a good and righteous man. The problem was that neither he nor I could understand why Jennifer left. This lack of understanding was the root of the pain. My bishop counseled me to move forward with my life and that, "Everything will be alright and will work out."

Over time, the miracle of the Atonement of Jesus Christ has healed me to the point that at times I almost feel as if the experience had never occurred. Yet at the time, I truly thought I would never recover. My burden has since been swept away to where I am no longer weighed down by it, though there is still occasional sadness.

Now I know that the Lord really does visit His people in their afflictions. I hope because of the sorrow and pain I experienced, that I am a better person, am kinder, and less judgmental.

Our sufferings can be so severe at times that it is easy to give up and lose faith in Heavenly Father. It is during the most difficult times that we must hold fast to our faith in the Lord. We can look to the examples of prophets in the scriptures who were humble and righteous to the end. Job's trials were almost too great to bear, but in the midst of all his suffering, Job declared, "Though he slay me, yet will I trust him: but I will maintain my own ways before him." (Job 13:15)

The Lord healed Job through the miracle of the Atonement of Jesus Christ. And if the Lord can heal Job, He can heal everyone else.

Mile Marker Seven: The Road to Peace Begins with Agency

Tim and Luke joined my carpool when I needed spiritual warriors by my side. They helped me realize that it doesn't matter what Mile Marker we're on, the road of mortality is an opportunity to use our agency to survive great loss and ultimately progress. Our Heavenly Father has great love for Tim and Luke. He also loves Donna and Jennifer, their ex-wives. Jesus Christ is continually looking after all parties involved in a divorce.

People don't enter marriage thinking, *"Hmm, I wonder if my fiancé is married to someone else"* or *"Gee whiz, my first divorce didn't give me enough opportunities for growth. I hope I can get remarried and be blindsided again so I can learn even more."* Satan tempts us to believe that if God loved us, He would prevent tragedies like bigamy, abandonment, and divorce. This convincing lie can be easy to believe when we see the collateral damage from divorce.

Others may say, "I didn't have any prior marriage experience and I'm still married. We both used our agency. Why couldn't you guys get it right?" Who says we have to get anything right the first time? Or the tenth? We are all in the driver's seat and there are no perfect drivers.

Prohibiting agency is Satan's plan, not God's. Luke and Tim watched their wives use their free will to end their marriages. That same gift of agency was used by both men to turn to the Lord and ask for the strength to let their wives go. Without free will there would be no personal growth. We would all be stagnant, never learning from our mistakes. Yet, the price tag for agency is immeasurable. How can spiritual progress be so important that God allows His children to abuse, deceive, hurt, and even kill each other? Isn't the cost of agency too great? No.

Jesus understood the cost and paid the price. He took up the cross to help us carry ours. Every pain suffered from divorce has been absorbed by the Atonement of Jesus Christ. The Lord must allow every survivor, and their ex-spouse, to fulfill their destiny so His judgments will be just.

From Tim and Luke I learned that:

- *Agency can be used to hurt or heal.*

- *Jesus Christ is continually feeling concern for all parties involved in divorce.*

- *Divorce presents opportunities to begin again with more experience.*

Questions

The same gift of agency that ended a marriage can be used to access healing from our Savior, Jesus Christ. What choices have you made to help heal your heart? Or to cause yourself more emotional pain?

_____
_____
_____
_____
_____

If you are divorced, it can be difficult to accept that the Lord loves and is concerned about your ex-spouse as much as He loves you. How do you feel when you think of the Lord's love for your ex-spouse? Why?

_____
_____
_____
_____
_____

What is the story you are telling yourself about your divorce-related experiences? How can you retell your story in a way that will allow you to heal faster and appreciate yourself on a higher level?

_____
_____
_____
_____
_____

Chapter Eight

The Crooked Path: Hannah's Detour

At church, there was a group of spunky retired ladies who sat together on the back row. When I walked by them one Sunday, I noticed Hannah. She was eighty-years-old, with stunning blue eyes, shimmery white hair, and an infectious smile. Hannah and I became friends and learned that we had much in common. She too, had navigated a difficult divorce. On Hannah's wedding day, sixty years earlier, she didn't have the courage to heed the promptings of the Spirit. Learning about Hannah's detour gave me more determination to never postpone a prompting.

Hannah's Story in Her Own Words

I started causing trouble for my parents in the womb. When I was born in 1936, my mother's uterus came out and they had to force it back in. After the delivery, Mother's health was so bad due to the complications of birth that she rarely held me as a baby. My father desperately wanted a son, and now they had four daughters. Mother was determined to please my father. Two years later, she almost lost her life in childbirth, but they finally got their son. Mother had all five of us in ten years and Daddy was so proud.

While learning to talk, I developed a stuttering problem and my siblings teased me mercilessly. They shut me down before I could express myself. I didn't want to be in situations where I'd be put on the spot, so I withdrew.

I was afraid of everything. When company came over, I hid outside by my favorite apple tree in the orchard. Once, we had a family picture taken and I wouldn't come down out of my tree. My parents left an empty seat in the picture and proudly displayed it in the living room for years. For me, it captured more than an image. It solidified my place in life—I was invisible.

Throughout my childhood, I didn't have a lot of physical affection from anyone. My mother was very prudish and proper; she rarely touched me. She struggled to show affection to her kids and continued her pattern of withholding love. From my perspective as a child, she only cared about Dad. Looking back, she loved us in her own way, but I never felt that love.

At age 3, my thirty-year-old uncle was babysitting my siblings and me. That night, I went to bed before anyone else. He followed me into my bedroom and touched me inappropriately. He said, "I love you and want to marry you. Will you wait for me? I'll be around when you grow up." I was starving for physical and emotional affection. I thought he was showing love. I didn't know I was being molested.

Due to my lack of appropriate physical contact with family members, my three-year-old self equated his touch with love. I told my mom what happened and my uncle never came back. Then I felt guilty. His absence solidified the idea in my mind that I wasn't worthy of being loved.

I was four-years-old when World War II broke out. It was a time of fear, political unrest, and families fighting to survive.

When our family became active in the Church, we lived in a little mining town in Idaho. We drove to church in the back of the old truck. I wanted the Church in my life, and to be a friend to Jesus. But I thought I was too bad to be His friend. I didn't know why I felt so ashamed of myself. I'd had so many negative messages given to me since the womb.

My daddy came home from work every day and listened to the radio. He was afraid the draft would force him to leave his family. If he became a farmer and bought animals he could avoid it, so that's exactly what he did. My parents purchased some cows and a large ranch. We girls worked on the farm like boys.

Growing up in the shadow of three accomplished older sisters was challenging. I always compared myself to them and felt like I didn't measure up. Being a teenager in the 50s as a young woman meant you learned to cook, sew, and excel at homemaking. One of my sisters was like my surrogate mother. She pushed me to do things before I was ready, resulting in failure.

As we hit puberty, we were known as the cutest girls in the Boise Valley. In time, I mostly overcame my stuttering problem and became a big flirt. As a teenager I was fickle, changing boyfriends once a month. I met my husband, Clarence, when I was 19. One Sunday at church, I felt him ogling me so I turned around and looked. He asked me if I needed a ride home. We went for a drive and began dating.

My older sister was a self-appointed matchmaker. It was a game for her to lie to get people together. She fibbed and told me my parents wanted me to marry Clarence. I thought they knew better than I did, so I better marry him.

Three months later, Clarence and I were on our way to the Idaho Falls temple to get married. On the way, he asked if I wanted to drive. I did, but I wasn't a good driver. He became enraged with my performance and called me stupid. No man had ever spoken to me that way before. I was humiliated. Dismayed, I sat in silence, wondering if I really wanted to get married.

When we arrived at the temple, we met up with family and friends. As I was dressing for the event, I quietly told my mother I didn't want to marry him.

She said, "Then we will stop the wedding right now and go home."

I said, "No, everyone is planning on a wedding and I don't want to spoil their plans."

For once my mother listened. Sadly, I didn't value myself enough to follow the prompting of the Spirit and call off my wedding.

We married and I learned more about Clarence's dysfunctional past. He had grown up in a very abusive home with a mother who had sexually abused him. His mother was dominated by a husband who was a womanizer. She carried on the family pattern and dominated her son. Clarence was scared of being rejected by his mother. He had a deep dislike for her as well. It was such an oxymoron. She came along on part of our honeymoon because she wanted to visit her brother, a foreshadowing of our future marriage. His mother always interfered and we let her.

As our marriage progressed, we had five children in nine years. Each pregnancy infuriated Clarence; he didn't want another mouth to feed.

When my daughter Susie was 7, I saw Clarence's father putting his hands down her panties. In horror, I retraced the past and suspected he had been doing it for years. When I found the courage to talk to his mother about it she said, "It's nothing. He touches all the girls." I was living a nightmare, always in fear of him coming over. In the 1960s, sexual abuse was brushed under the carpet; it wasn't viewed as a big thing. It never entered my mind to press charges.

My husband often called me a whore. Because of the negative

messages he sent me, I felt insecure about myself and wanted to cover up. One day he bought me a sexy swimsuit with different colors of brown. I tried it on and he said, "You look like a chocolate cake." That was the only compliment he paid me in twenty years. I still remember it fifty years later.

Half-way through our marriage, Clarence brought home a book for me to read and wanted me to implement it in our marriage. It was about happy homemakers who took care of their families by day and became prostitutes by night. I was completely shocked and disgusted. Luckily, I valued myself enough to refuse his proposal. He viewed me as a whore even though I had been completely faithful to him during our entire marriage.

When we got married, I was overly sensitive. We were two fractured souls coming from dysfunctional families. We knew nothing about healthy communication. With such a lack of intimacy, communication, and trust, I developed a deep hurt in my heart.

My husband began to physically hurt me after our fifth child was born. One day, I was washing the car when he started beating me with the washing implement. Quickly, I ran into the house and hid behind the children to avoid his rage. Never knowing what would trigger his angry tirades or physical abuse, I lived my life walking on eggshells.

Clarence resented the children and often hit them with his knuckles on top of their heads—hard. I pleaded with him to stop while screaming inside. I used to cry a lot and he'd sarcastically say, "I'm glad you're crying, I wish you'd cry all the time." Over time, I learned to block out the negative messages. I decided never to cry again, and I didn't for many years.

Fits of terror were familiar events throughout our marriage. Clarence had epilepsy and stress would invoke seizures. When he verbally abused me, I'd come back with one-liners that nailed him to the wall. He would pout, get angry, and then have a seizure.

My husband wanted to control every part of my life. He didn't want me getting close to people. Whenever I started making friends, he cut off my support systems by demanding we relocate. We moved almost every year of our marriage for twenty-two years. It was exhausting.

For days, I pondered and prayed fervently to receive personal revelation. I didn't want to live in turmoil for the rest of my life. The Holy Ghost told me to have faith in myself and make decisions. Through all of the pain, it never entered my mind to blame God. Instead, I viewed him as a compassionate Father in Heaven, and longed to be close to Him and His son Jesus Christ. I continued to pray to God, asking Him to share all of my burdens. Putting my energy into loving and teaching our children helped to heal my heart.

I went on a temple trip with some of my supportive church friends. When I came home, Clarence was in his usual enraged state. He was cursing at me, the temple, and the prophet. It was devastating. Right then, I made my decision. After buckets of tears, twenty-two years, twenty-two moves, and five children, I found an attorney the next day and filed for divorce.

Going to church was interesting. One member of our ward hissed at me when he learned I was getting divorced. In spite of opposition, there were also kind ward members who stood by me. An older, married Elder was Christ-like and counseled with me. I felt no judgment from him. He helped me realize I was a good person and I couldn't make the marriage work by myself.

Clarence had pounded into my head that I was stupid and incapable. Pushing past that mentality was difficult. The next weekend I had a yard sale and earned six hundred dollars, enough to buy my own car. That was liberating. I packed up our two youngest sons, ages 12 and 15, and drove to Utah. Our boys were supportive of me.

We arrived in Provo early in the morning. By noon, I had secured a job in a sewing factory. That day, we found living quarters and the boys enrolled in school. I had enough money to pay for hot lunches and enough bread, peanut butter, and milk to feed us until I got paid in two weeks. Clarence paid his child support on time every month and I was grateful. The Lord loved me and was helping us. We made friends with the landlady, who had us over for dinner.

In spite of the abuse and the heartache stemming from my marriage, I still believed in the Gospel of Jesus Christ. I didn't work to receive faith; it was a spiritual gift given to me at birth. God gave me gospel roots that remained firmly planted as I took my children to church and taught them the Gospel in my home. I chose *not* to let go of my faith.

The Lord warned me about marrying Clarence and I did it anyway. I felt intense sorrow for ignoring the warning signs. During the years of verbal and physical abuse I promised myself I would never cry again. Ten years later, I was in counseling when tears actually welled up in my eyes. I realized I hadn't cried for a decade.

When our youngest son was engaged to be married, I was still struggling with all of the abuse I had endured in my former marriage. I knew that seeing Clarence at our son's wedding reception would trigger anxiety and I did not want him to attend. Stuck in the pain of the past, I couldn't move forward until the Savior helped me. One day, I was pondering the Atonement of Christ as I stared at a picture of Jesus on the wall. As I looked at

Him, He seemed to say, "Hannah, I atoned for Clarence too." That was a defining moment for me. It was true.

At the wedding, I had worked through my feelings enough to sit at the same table with Clarence. In spite of many dark days, I came out smiling.

Years later, when Clarence was still living, I woke up and was inspired to write his eulogy. I focused on the many good things he did during his teaching career. We always had a nice home and our material needs were met; I acknowledged him as a good provider.

Today, it's easy to forgive him when I see my beautiful children and grandchildren. My sons wouldn't be who they are without him. My lovely daughter would not be the person she is. There are blessings in every challenge, even in divorce. When you allow the enabling power of the Savior's Atonement to make up the difference for you and your former spouse, *eventually* you forget the pain.

There was a lot of heartache during those long years of healing. At times I didn't know if I would ever recover—but I did. God blesses us abundantly, then turns around and blesses us some more.

We have an awesome God.

Mile Marker Eight: Slow Down and Yield to the Spirit

As I carpooled with Hannah, our journey together taught me to slow down and yield to the Spirit. In my former marriage, I used my agency to focus on thoughts that destroyed my peace. Hannah inspired me to invite the Spirit to be the driving force in my life, focusing on the Savior, and then the toughie, letting go of the outcome. This concept requires a mighty surrender.

In *The Book of Mormon*, Nephi was a righteous prophet who was highly favored of the Lord. Yet, he suffered physical, emotional, and verbal abuse from his brothers. Nephi got worn down—he had some serious questions. It's comforting to know that even prophets ask why. The following scriptures show his humanness when he, too, yielded to sin:

"And why should I *yield* to sin, because of my flesh? Yea, why should I give way to temptations, that the evil one have place in my heart to destroy my peace and afflict my soul? Why am I angry because of mine enemy? Awake, my soul! No longer droop in sin. Rejoice, O my heart, and give place no more for the enemy of my soul." (2 Nephi 4:27-28, emphasis added)

When Nephi chose to yield to the Spirit instead of Satan, he realized that his own thoughts about his brothers led to *his* feelings. *He* was responsible for his anger and lack of peace—not his abusive brothers. A spiritual wakeup call shifted the momentum of his thoughts.

Even prophets aren't perfect. We grow into accountability which requires lots of practice. The Lord is keenly aware of our efforts, He rewards us every time we try. A failed marriage doesn't mean we are failures—but it can feel that way. Learning to control our thoughts brings spiritual power. The Atonement of Jesus Christ covers all of the pain associated with divorce. As our healing continues, obedience brings confidence and invites the Spirit into our lives.

"When we feel the Spirit, we can be assured that God, in that very moment, is aware of all our personal circumstances and is supporting us in every way." (Spencer Campbell)

Through Hannah's experiences I learned that:

- *Learning to yield to the Spirit takes practice—even for prophets.*

- *We grow into accountability.*

- *Inviting the Spirit to be the driving force in my life will help me let go of the outcome.*

Questions

Read 2 Nephi Chapter 4. What insights did Nephi receive during his wake-up call to yield to the Spirit? After you study, pray in faith and ask the Lord how to more fully yield your will to His.

_____
_____
_____
_____
_____

We grow into accountability. How has your divorce, or the divorce of a family member or friend, affected your desire to be accountable to the Lord? Have you become more or less accountable? Take the time for an honest assessment.

_____
_____
_____
_____
_____

When we feel the Spirit, God is reassuring us of His desire to help us and His awareness of our circumstances. What specific things can you do to invite the Spirit to help you let go of unmet expectations and accept unwanted outcomes?

_____
_____
_____
_____
_____

Chapter Nine

Warning Signs: Hannah's Redemption

After Hannah's divorce from Clarence, she rebounded into a second marriage. Her new spouse had many secrets. After several years of marriage, the horrific crimes committed by her husband came to light. Hannah felt like she was stuck in a nightmare with her life spinning out of control. Her anger began to grow and soon she wanted her husband dead. In desperation, she slowed down and focused on the Savior who helped save her from herself. Without the enabling power of the Atonement of Jesus Christ, she believes she would have committed murder. Hannah's experiences helped me look to the Lord.

Hannah's Story in Her Own Words

When I divorced Clarence, I had allowed myself to be stripped of all dignity as a woman. I promised myself that I wasn't going to allow my angry ex-husband to break me—but I was broken. I used to tell myself, "I love you, Hannah," even though I didn't believe it. Day-to-day tasks were unbearable, even a simple shopping trip was paralyzing. In agony, I walked through the aisles with my head down, hoping to melt into the floor.

Being a single mom in the 70s was difficult; divorce was almost taboo. I didn't know why I still believed in marriage, but I wanted so much to be cherished by a man.

When I met Lane, I had been alone for four months. He was

newly divorced, had been single for a year, and he came with a perfect resume. He was handsome, charming, and on the prowl for a wife. Lane was a family man, active in the Church, fulfilled his church callings, and attended the temple.

Lane was determined to show me how spiritual he was. Every kind thing he said was like manna to my starving soul. I was so smitten by his charm I couldn't see who he really was. One night he drove me to a romantic spot by the Provo temple. He rattled off spiritual doctrine and impressed me with his knowledge, all by the light of the stars.

When we met, I was an empty well and he began filling me up. Lane showered me with compliments and praise. I was charmed by the thought of having a faithful eternal companion and he was available. During our courtship, he bought me diamonds and rubies. He paid attention to my children and bought them gifts. Desperately wanting to be loved, I married on the rebound. I drove full speed ahead into a second marriage.

Lane was an electrician. Early in our marriage, he talked about the ease of swindling people he worked with. This was the first warning sign about his true character and I ignored it. The fact that he kept thinking about cheating people showed what was in his heart. At first, I thought he was joking around. I had no idea what kind of man he was or the temptations he dealt with. Satan saw his weaknesses and wanted to take him down.

Lane was viewing pornography and hiding magazines on the sly. He always wanted to do service projects for families that had young girls. Lane would spend hours at their houses, taking lots of time to get to know the family. Then he would volunteer to babysit the girls by himself. He had spent so much time with the family that they learned to trust him. I would offer to help babysit with Lane but he always refused. I should have recognized his behavior as a warning sign.

Unexpectedly, Lane decided to get his electrical license in Oregon, which meant frequent trips from Idaho to Oregon for schooling. My daughter Corinne lived there and we were always welcomed into her home. We enjoyed many lovely visits with the family. Lane had a special interest in Corinne's six-year-old girl, Tana. He doted on her and bought her gifts. We visited often to play with the kids and babysit. I was so happy that he loved my daughter and grand kids.

One holiday, Corinne was in town for a visit at our home. That evening, she wanted the children to sleep upstairs in the guest bedroom with her. Lane insisted they sleep alone in the basement so Corinne could get more rest. They settled in for the evening, and a few hours later Corinne felt a prompting to have the children come upstairs and sleep in her room. When they were safely tucked in bed, her daughter, Tana, spoke the haunting words that changed us forever.

"Mommy, Grandpa has been touching me."

"What did you say, Tana?"

"Grandpa touches me whenever we are together."

"Oh, Tana . . ." As her daughter spoke the unspeakable, Corinne ordered herself to stay calm. She said a silent prayer, asking God to help her know what to say.

"What else happened, Tana?"

Corinne's courageous daughter began describing unspeakable acts.

"You are so brave for telling the truth, Tana. I love you."

Emotions flooded her being as she frantically searched her mind for proof that it wasn't true. *This happens to other families, not mine. I am a good mother, I protect my kids!*

Corinne was reeling from shock. She made a mental note to never let Tana out of her sight again—ever.

Corinne spent the night mentally dissecting Lane's interactions with her daughter. It was like putting together a thousand-piece puzzle; each tiny piece a warning sign. Guilt and heartache overtook her mind and body. Lane had appeared to be an upstanding member of the Church, loving and kind. Corinne curled up in the fetal position, praying to disappear. She never imagined he was capable of committing such horrific crimes to a child—her child.

Corrine didn't sleep that night and wondered if she would ever sleep again.

When the sun came up, Corinne wasn't sure how to handle the situation. Her heart told her to believe Tana. The Holy Ghost whispered, "It's true." The next morning Corinne called my bishop and told him what happened, asking him to speak with Lane immediately. She wanted Lane to be the one to tell me, to look me in the eye and be accountable for his crimes.

The next morning, I walked into the kitchen to start breakfast for the family. Corinne stumbled in and looked at me dead on. Her blood shot eyes and heavy countenance caused my internal alarm to go off. What was going on; had I offended her? Never before had I seen the look of pain on her face that stared back at me.

"What's wrong, honey?" I asked.

Corinne nodded her head, unable to speak. Without a word, she packed up the children and drove home. A feeling of doom was mounting in my chest—I was baffled and hurt. When she arrived home, she called and asked if Lane had told me anything. I said no, and asked her what she was talking about. Silence on the other end—then she said goodbye. Panic set in and a premonition in my heart started preparing me, but my mind wouldn't accept it.

The next day the bishop came to our house. I invited him in and began asking him questions. Instead of addressing my concerns, he and Lane went to the basement to talk. Quietly, I tiptoed to the bottom of the stairs and heard the bishop ask Lane if he had molested Tana. He said, "Yes." I nearly dropped to the ground.

Terror wracked my mind—I couldn't believe it. How was this possible? I imagined the bishop was in shock like me. Lane was the center of our ward, always willing to help. The bishop must have been shaken, and I was stunned beyond description.

Wrapping my head around the situation was hopeless. I rationalized what I was hearing; it had to be a mistake. Almost unconsciously, I climbed the stairs and collapsed into bed, emotionally and physically numb. Hours later, Lane came into our room. It was not possible that my husband had abused Tana—I refused to believe it.

The next day Corinne called and said, "Mom, Lane molests girls." I was in shock, but deep down I knew it was true. My initial reactions turned to anger, almost rage. I wanted Lane in jail. The warning signs had surrounded me, but I wouldn't yield to the Spirit. Swindling people, the hidden magazines, the obsession with my granddaughter—I was sick.

Corinne called the police in her State and they contacted the authorities where we lived. I met with the officers and signed a paper saying Lane had sexually abused my granddaughter.

The next few weeks were terrible. The pressure was palpable and the day of reckoning came. In the courtroom, I was shocked to hear my husband plead guilty. I was surprised by the small glimmer of hope I had that he would truly repent. Within minutes, the glimmer was gone.

Lane was only sentenced for three months to a halfway house. He could work during the day and was locked up at night. The leniency of the sentence did not fit the crime. Lane felt sorry for himself—what a joke. He would be wandering the streets; I was horrified. I wanted them to lock him up and throw away the key.

Several years earlier in our marriage, Lane had purchased a gun for me to use for protection. After the hearing he said, "Now that I'm going to the halfway house, you can use your gun to protect yourself." I thought, *protect myself from whom? From you—you're the one I need protection from. I'll kill you, you son of a gun.*

Lane had lied for so long, he could no longer tell the difference between lies and truth. After the trial, I drove alone to my shattered home. We had a picture of Christ on the wall in our living room. I looked at the picture and told Jesus, "The Church isn't true." The Holy Spirit answered, "The Church is true." I refused to believe.

I lost my husband and gave up on the Church the same day. The Holy Ghost had lovingly and carefully placed warning signs before me, telling me to slow down, listen, and to trust my inner voice. Instead of yielding to the Spirit, I ignored the promptings.

While Lane labored in the community during his three-month "sentence," he convinced many people that he had been set up by my daughter and me. Even though he had admitted his crime, he convinced people he was innocent. In their eyes, he was the "perfect" Christian: always serving, responsible, compassionate, and trustworthy. It was too painful for members of the community as a whole to believe they had been duped. Facing the truth about a child molester living in their midst for years was unthinkable. It was easier for them to ignore the warning signs like I had.

I wanted Lane dead.

While I entertained thoughts of killing him, I didn't realize I was premeditating murder because I didn't have a set plan. Thank God the chance never came. The horror of my husband's abuse of my granddaughter, and possibly many other young girls, was unbearable. Twice I was married in the temple, and twice betrayed by both husbands.

While Lane was in the halfway house, I mechanically went through the motions of each day. It felt like I was living someone else's life. Three months ended and before I knew it, he had fulfilled his sentence. It was a Saturday night when he was released. Dramatically, he declared his deep commitment to the Church. I wanted to vomit.

My testimony became weak because I let the constant stress wear it down. I detested men and realized that I hated half of the people on the planet. I asked God, "Are you like the other men I've known in my life? I know you're not but it feels like all men are jerks." I had become accustomed to picking on men, so I started picking on God, too.

Months of despair went by. One day, in my anguish, I humbled myself and read an *Ensign* magazine article. It spoke of Jesus Christ atoning for our heartaches and emotions as well as our sins. I thought to myself, "I've really got heartache; will I ever find any relief?"

After nine months of being filled with hatred, I realized that my anger was destroying me—not Lane. Wanting to be free from the rage, I humbled myself and prayed that God would take away my desire to kill my husband. Immediately, I felt relief.

As I called upon Jesus Christ in my moment of despair, I felt the enabling power of His Atonement. I promised the Lord I would not think about killing Lane anymore if He would take away the pain enough for me to bear it. I made a solemn promise to the Lord and felt Him make a promise to me. It was as serious as a baptismal covenant. While calling upon my Savior, He began carrying the burden with me. I had been trying to bear it alone and the weight was crushing. Why hadn't I turned to Him sooner?

That terrible time was a long journey shrouded with dark clouds of despair. I wondered at times, *what's the use?* But the Lord kept

His promises and carried me through. Finally, my divorce finalized and I was legally free from Lane.

People would tell me, "If I'd gone through what you had, I would have quit the Church." I learned that the Gospel of Jesus Christ was true, but some followers make bad choices.

Through it all, the Savior continued to show His love for me. Eventually, my pleadings for a good husband were realized. A year after my divorce, I met Tom, a kind and honorable man. We courted for a long time and he finally convinced me to marry him. We are still married today. It hasn't always been easy, but Tom has been a good husband and carpool companion. He has loved me through the hurt and pain as I headed down my road of healing.

At age 70, ten years into my third marriage, the doctors discovered a tumor in the bone surrounding my brain. It was removed, and I hit another low point as my mortality weighed on me. I was seriously ill and had to stay in the hospital. The brain tumor forced me to slow down and gave me the opportunity to yield to the Spirit. Instead of fighting to live, life had beaten me down so much I was not sure if I cared.

For many years after I married Tom, I was upset with myself. I felt guilty that I had spent so many years of my life not valuing me. Since then I have learned that when we don't love ourselves, we have signs on our door saying: *Bait me; I'm worthless; do what you will with me; I'm not worthy of any good things; wipe your feet on my doormat and I'll happily clean it up.*

Day after day, I would lie in my hospital bed telling myself I deserved all the bad things that had happened to me. I had hated myself for so long, I didn't know how to stop. I was God's child, but I had forgotten why that mattered. My pride got in the way and I tried to shut the Savior out of my life. Jesus was there with His arms outstretched, waiting for me to accept His embrace. Without accessing the enabling power of Jesus Christ, I was stranded.

Secretly, I hoped my life would end, but God had other plans. He wanted me to repent.

Over time, I became humble enough to do an inventory of my life. I began the repentance process. For a month, I lay in the hospital bed with a prayer in my heart saying, "Heavenly Father, I'm so sorry for everything I've done." With repentance came the pains of a tortured soul. For the first time, I became fully accountable to God for all of my own actions, instead of focusing on the sins and misdeeds of my ex-husbands and others.

Day and night, I lay in pain and talked to the Lord. As I pondered the Atonement of Jesus Christ, I began to understand what Jesus did for me personally. Until that time, I didn't understand Christ's Atonement or how to apply it to my life. When I realized I had to be willing to receive His comfort by exercising faith in my Savior, Jesus Christ, everything changed. It became clear to me that the Holy Spirit was a gift from my loving Heavenly Father, given to protect my family and me. Until I allowed the Lord to help me, I was stranded.

I felt intense sorrow for ignoring the warning signs. As a young adult, the Lord warned me about marrying my first husband, Clarence, and I did it anyway. Our journey was difficult and it ended in divorce. Determined to marry on the rebound, I didn't allow myself enough time for personal growth between relationships.

After I married Lane, there were signs everywhere about his inappropriate behavior with women and children. It was easier to ignore them than face the truth. People would ask me why I didn't figure out what Lane was doing. Suspecting my husband to be a child molester was as crazy as saying he was going to fly to the moon. When I made covenants to love and cherish Lane, I put my life in his hands. I was deceived.

Regardless of what an ex-spouse has done, if we want to forgive, we must repent. Even after a full repentance, I repeatedly said I was sorry to the Lord until the Spirit finally told me to knock it off. Satan wanted me to suffer endlessly. When I was unable to forgive myself, Jesus spoke my language until I finally understood. Repenting unlocked the most important secret of my life: The key to forgiveness is repentance.

I learned that the Lord's infinite sacrifice was for me personally. His Atonement made it possible for me to repent and become clean again. After I had suffered for my own sins, with a truly penitent heart, my suffering was swallowed up in the Atonement of Jesus Christ.

Allowing yourself to feel relief, even when things aren't fully resolved, will be one of the greatest gifts you can give yourself. Through these experiences the Lord taught me to quit beating myself up. The beautiful peace from His Spirit permeated my being. Finally, I was good with God.

I learned a life-changing lesson: In order to fully forgive, I had to repent.

Looking back with perspective, I recognize the foolishness of children—and we are all children. I can even laugh about some of the horrible things that happened to me, just as I can laugh at the pranks my kids used to pull. Not that it wasn't serious, but because life is too short. We must find a way to experience joy in the journey.

Mile Marker Nine: Let Christ Be Your Compass

Hannah endured the heart wrenching reality that her husband had sexually abused her granddaughter. Because of her husband's choices, she was forced to think the unthinkable. Abuse in many forms deeply affects many families of divorce, shattering hearts and homes. The aftermath can be traumatizing on so many levels. The agony can only be swallowed up by our Savior, Jesus Christ. His infinite Atonement will encompass all aspects of our healing.

The magnetic needle in a compass always points north, aligning itself with the top of the earth's magnetic field. Just like that magnetic needle, we have an internal compass pointing toward Christ. He is in perfect alignment with Heavenly Father and we can always trust His guidance. When we are out of alignment, Jesus Christ will direct us toward a path of peace.

Elder Richard G. Scott provides powerful perspective:

"Satan will strive to alienate you from your Father in Heaven with the thought that if He loved you He would have prevented the tragedy. Do not be kept from the very source of true healing by the craftiness of the prince of evil and his wicked lies. Recognize that if you have feelings that you are not loved by your Father in Heaven, you are being manipulated by Satan. Even when it may seem very difficult to pray, kneel and ask Father in Heaven to give you the capacity to trust Him and to feel His love for you. Ask to come to know that His Son can heal you through His merciful Atonement. While an important part of healing, if the thought of forgiveness causes you yet more pain, set that step aside until you have more experience with the Savior's healing power in your life." (Richard G. Scott, "To Heal the Shattering Consequences of Abuse," *Ensign*, May 2008, p. 42)

When thoughts of forgiveness cause more pain, Elder Scott has encouraged us to put that step aside, and develop a closer relationship with the Savior. There is no timetable for healing.

From Hannah's experiences I learned:

- *When thoughts of forgiveness cause pain, focus on my relationship with the Savior.*

- *A failed marriage does not mean I am a failure.*

- *Repentance is the key to forgiveness.*

QUESTIONS

Have you ever been abused, or did you abuse your spouse in a former marriage? How can experience with the Savior and His Atonement help all parties affected by abuse? How did Jesus handle abuse?

_____
_____
_____
_____
_____

Do you feel like a failure because of your divorce? Or the divorce of someone close to you? Why or why not? How can you be more gentle with yourself and develop a habit of owning your successes? Make a list of your accomplishments.

_____
_____
_____
_____
_____

Repentance being the key to forgiveness can feel counterintuitive. Have you ever explored this principle? Record what you need to repent of in order to forgive yourself, another, or an ex-spouse.

_____
_____
_____
_____
_____

Chapter Ten

Sarah's Journey: Ben's Life Saving Prompting

When I first met Sarah, she appeared to have a perfect life. Her stylish brown hair that matched her eyes always looked fabulous. I was amazed by her ability to organize her home, take care of her family, and fulfill her church responsibilities. What would it be like to have it all together like her? Inside, I didn't realize I was struggling with the pride of comparison. One Thanksgiving morning, I went on a walk and saw Sarah. She asked about my holiday, and I told her about my book project. When I said the words *divorce* and *survivor*, Sarah became interested. As our friendship grew, I was stunned to learn that this "super mom" had previously gone through a devastating divorce and almost took her own life.

Sarah's Story in Her Own Words

After four years of dating, I married my high school sweetheart in the Salt Lake Temple. I loved Sam more than life itself; he was truly my soul mate. Leaving my family and friends in Utah to join him while he fulfilled his full-time military duty in California was difficult, but I loved him so much I was willing to sacrifice. During the first two years of our marriage, he was deployed more than he was home. It was torture being apart, but after several deployments, he finally got an office job and we were able to be together.

Working full-time for a wonderful company was fulfilling. Because of my hard work, I was awarded a leadership scholarship to a local college. In the evenings, we both took college classes. We made a great life for ourselves as a young couple starting out—or so I thought.

Something caused a shift in our relationship and Sam became unavailable. I spent months of sleepless nights wondering if he would come home drunk, or at all.

Then he stopped touching me. Heartbroken, I tried to understand why he didn't want to be intimate or acknowledge me, but he was unwilling to talk. I felt invisible.

One day, everything changed. Sam informed me he didn't want to be a member of The Church of Jesus Christ of Latter-day Saints. He didn't believe in the doctrine and would no longer be attending church. He decided he could no longer live his life the way he had in the past and still be happy.

Heartsick, I reassured him of my commitment. He was still the most important person in my life. Somehow, we would work through these changes. I still believed we were meant to be together forever. Several months later, Sam came home from work, packed a bag of personal belongings and said, "I want a divorce and I don't have to give you a reason why." My mind was reeling, searching for answers.

Sam disappeared. He walked out the door and left me standing alone in our apartment. I didn't know how to contact him. As my world came crashing down on me, I felt totally hopeless. When I called friends and family, no one knew anything about Sam's whereabouts. I contacted his commanding officer in the military, explained the situation, and finally reached him.

I told Sam I would give him thirty days to make sure he wanted a divorce. At the end of that time, he reassured me he hadn't changed his mind. We had been married for four years and been together for eight. Why would he want to give up on us? Nothing made sense.

Sam had been living a double life. All of the signs were there, but I refused to see them. I had ignored my "gut feeling" that something was wrong. When I started digging, I found out he had been having an affair with a young college student. Now I had a valid reason to leave. I quit my job, dropped out of college, and packed up the fairytale life I thought I'd had. Desperate for the love of my family to help me through this devastating time, I moved back to Utah.

My dad, Mario, bought a condo and let me rent it from him while I sorted out the broken pieces of my life. I had only been settled back in Utah for three weeks when another bombshell went off. A letter came in the mail saying that Sam had to provide blood tests in a paternity case regarding a seven-year-old that might be Sam's child.

My heart stopped. The numbness quickly spread throughout my body. To find out Sam might have a child with another woman almost threw me over the edge. I had only begun to comprehend the years of lies and deceit.

The results of the paternity test came back positive. I collapsed when I learned that my husband had a seven-year-old daughter. While Sam was dating me in high school, he had gotten another girl pregnant. Sam had reconnected with his daughter and her mother and decided he wanted them back in his life. We were going through divorce proceedings when I found out they were expecting another child together, while I was still his wife.

Wrapping my head around this outrageous news was nearly impossible. I had married someone in the temple who was involved in a scandalous life. He continued to violate his covenants while still married to me. My life had become a freak show.

Over the following months, I tried to accept the loss of my husband and my dreams for our future family. We hadn't had children yet, but I had looked forward to being a mother. I had been faithful to my husband and true to our covenants. Desperate to know I was worthy of being loved by a man, I tried to convince myself I was not a failure.

Once our divorce was final, I decided to be brave and start dating. A returned missionary asked me out and I was excited for our first date. I felt I should be honest and upfront, so I informed him that I had been married before and was recently divorced. He called me up the next day and said, "I cannot date a girl who has been used. I'm sorry, but I'll have to cancel our date."

I hit rock bottom.

My heart could not handle the cruelty of the returned missionary's comments. I stopped going to church and spent every moment I wasn't at work trying to "sleep" away the anguish. Feeling hopeless, I prayed to God and begged him to make my heart stop hurting. Desperate for relief, I told Him I could not take anymore. I hated my life and wasn't strong enough to live one more day with such cutting pain. Who will ever want me?

My soul was so full of despair it felt like I could physically reach inside my body and grab hold of the pain. It hurt so bad it felt tangible. I had never known a lower point in my life.

I decided to end the pain.

That night, when I came home from work, I parked my car in the garage, locked up my house, and shut the blinds. While searching for every prescription and non-prescription drug I had in the cupboards, I got a glass of water, knelt down by the side of my bed, and begged God to forgive me. Then I grabbed a handful of pills.

As I was about to swallow, the doorbell rang. Quietly waiting, I didn't get up to answer it, but the person started knocking. I became very agitated while waiting for the noise to stop. Relentless knocking turned into bell ringing, followed by pebbles thrown at the window. Peeking through the blinds, I saw Ben, a very good friend of mine whom I had known for years.

Why is he at my house? I hadn't shown any signs of how low I really was to my family or friends. I hadn't seen Ben in months and had no idea why he would show up now. I was not going to answer the door, but he would not leave.

I kept thinking, *Why are you still here? My car is in the garage and the blinds are shut. Don't you realize I'm not home?*

After thirty minutes, I finally swung open the door.

"What are you doing here?" I asked.

He replied, "I don't know, Sarah, you tell me. I was on my way home from work and felt strongly that I should drive by and check on you. Are you okay?"

The lump in my throat was enormous—I couldn't speak. I invited him in and ran upstairs to my room. I scooped up the pills, and flushed them down the toilet. My emotions were raw and I spent the next several hours crying as he comforted me. It was too painful to talk.

After that dark day, I knew Heavenly Father loved me. He did not take away my pain or heartache, but He sent Ben, a living angel, to hold me. With that knowledge, I knew that in time my wounds would heal. Because of such a profound experience, I knew God loved me and was aware of me as an individual. He would pick me up whenever I felt weak, alone, or afraid.

A short time later, Heavenly Father sent my sweet loving dad to lift my spirits. He had lived out of State most of my life. Although he and my mother divorced when I was only three, we were still very close. I could tell him anything and he would respond without criticism or judgment. He was always there for me with a listening ear, offering wisdom and advice.

One day, during his trip to Utah, we went to a pond. This was a place I frequently visited to feed the ducks and think. I always found peace staring at the water and listening to the sounds of nature. When we reached the water, I threw pieces of bread to the birds. A female duck lay in the sand near the water. Several others were pecking at her. She was an ugly mutant duck with no feathers on her head or down her neck. Blood oozed from her body. She was so weak she could barely lift her head; she made no sound at all. She was dying, and the other ducks wouldn't leave her alone. They pecked at her until I couldn't stand to watch any longer.

I finally said, "Dad, go get her."

He replied, "Sarah, it is nature taking its course; it's survival of the fittest. The duck must be sick and I don't want to touch it."

I begged him to go and get the duck.

"Please don't let her die, Dad—we can save her."

My sweet dad grabbed an old rug out of the trunk of the car and carefully walked down the steep hill to where the duck was lying. He shooed the other ducks away and tenderly wrapped her in the rug and carried her to me. She tried to peck at us but was too weak. I held her all the way to my grandma's house where Dad was staying. We put her in a box for the night. If she lived until morning, I could keep her until she was well enough to be released into the wild.

I thought about the ugly duck all night long—it felt as if I was the mutant duck. She and I were going through the same pain together. We had both been rejected and needed someone to help us and hold us until we were strong enough to walk on our own. Throughout the night, I prayed for the duck to live. I wanted her to have the opportunity to heal and not hurt anymore.

The next morning, I drove to my grandma's house and ran to the back patio. To my surprise, the duck was standing up by herself.

She was scared and shivering, but she was alive. Dad was gently spraying the dried blood off her with the hose. He let me take her back to my condo and nurse her back to health. The front patio of my condo was enclosed, so I could leave her there safely during the day. We bought a kiddy pool for her to swim and bathe in. I made her a bed in a cardboard box and fed her antibiotic duck feed. Slowly, but surely, she began to heal.

My duck had lain down and prepared to die—just as I had the day I almost killed myself. God gave me another chance at life by sending Ben to my home. He picked me up and carried me to safety. When I was strong enough, Heavenly Father gently helped me stand on my own two feet. I was determined to do the same for my little friend.

For three months, I nursed the sweet duck back to health. I kept her box clean, the patio sprayed off, and gave her fresh food and water every day. She would sit by me on the front steps and we spent a lot of time together. We learned to relate to one another, to trust. When she was strong enough to be set free, she was eating out of my hand.

The day I set her free was unforgettable. I took her to a different pond than where she used to live. Hesitantly, she walked out of her box onto the sand by the water. She looked around, too nervous to take another step. Then she waddled over to the water and started to paddle around a small area of the pond.

I stayed with her until she was swimming all over the pond. Finally, I knew she was safe and would be okay. Several times a week, for a few months, I returned to the pond. I recognized her by the hole in one of her webbed feet. She always waddled up to me and ate from my hand, still trusting and grateful someone cared enough to give her another chance at life. Like me, she had to start over in a new home with new friends, but finally she was strong enough to survive.

Two years later, I remarried a wonderful man named Tom. At my wedding, I told Ben the truth about that fateful night—that because of him I was given another chance at life and love. I will forever be in his debt for listening to the Spirit that led him to my doorstep. He heard the promptings of the Holy Ghost and heeded the guidance of the Lord. I love Ben for caring enough about me to help me to not give up on my life.

I have now been married for eighteen years and have been blessed with five precious children. The journey has not been easy, but it *has* been worth it.

The best part of my story is about forgiveness. It took two years after my divorce before I stopped feeling the heartache every single day. I had lots of good days, and not every day was horrible, but there was always a feeling of loneliness nagging at my heart.

One morning, I woke up and noticed the feeling was gone, the heartache was not there. It had disappeared. I would still have sad moments when I would feel bad for a minute or two, but the sorrow had left me and I knew the Lord was healing me from the inside out.

Two years after my divorce was final, I experienced one of my greatest memories from that time period. I got a phone call at work with a familiar voice on the other end.

"Hi, Sarah . . . do you know who this is?"

"Of course, I do. Hello, Sam, how are you?"

He replied, "Do you remember the day I left? There was something you said to me, Sarah, and it always stuck. You said that what goes around comes around, and someday I would experience an ounce of the pain I caused you in your life. Do you remember saying that?"

"Yes, of course I do, I would never forget a second of that day."

"Well, you were right."

Sam told me the story of a pretty rough full-circle experience he had recently gone through. His wife had abandoned him, and now he understood my pain. We both apologized for any hurt, pain or suffering we'd caused each other. We genuinely forgave each other entirely. The burden—the sack of anger, hate, betrayal, and bitterness—fell from my back and I was set free from the prison of heartache. I knew in my heart I had completely forgiven him.

I hung up the phone with a smile on my face and warmth in my heart. The most miraculous feeling of peace, contentment, love, and hope came over me like I have never felt before. Sam and I still keep in touch a couple of times a year and will always remain friends.

Forgiveness is one of the greatest blessings our Savior has given us. Because of His Atonement, we can eventually feel peace and happiness in our hearts and souls after divorce. His all-encompassing love and sacrifice for us makes it possible for us to repent, living a life free of guilt, grudge, and hate. I love Him for all He has given to me in my life—especially for the hard times which have only made me stronger. Jesus Christ is my miracle.

Mile Marker Ten: Tune into Kindness

My journey with Sarah taught me a profound lesson: The pride of comparison is spiritually dangerous. Without thinking, I had compared myself to Sarah. Similarly, the returned missionary compared Sarah to other young women who hadn't been divorced. Making comparisons can send us and others down a dead-end road.

It's easy to say, "Let rude comments roll off like water on a duck's back." When someone is wounded by a divorce, at times it is impossible to be that strong. When harsh comments took Sarah to her lowest point, she needed a rescuer. Ben, another returned missionary, acted as a true Christian. He cared about Sarah instead of comparing her to other divorced women. His faithful response to a prompting evokes a special feeling of gratitude for the mercy and grace of our Heavenly Father and His son, Jesus Christ, our deliverer.

Tragically, divorce can create heartache that is so deep that precious lives are taken through suicide. For those suffering from this tragedy, Bruce R. McConkie shared the following:

"Suicide consists in the voluntary and intentional taking of one's own life, particularly where the person involved is accountable and has a sound mind . . . *Persons subject to great stresses may lose control of themselves and become mentally clouded to the point that they are no longer accountable for their acts.* Such are not to be condemned for taking their own lives. It should also be remembered that judgment is the Lord's. He knows the thoughts, intents, and abilities of men; and He in His infinite wisdom will make all things right in due course." (*Mormon Doctrine*, Salt Lake City: Bookcraft, 1966, p. 771; emphasis added)

These comforting words confirm the merciful nature of our Savior, Jesus Christ. Thankfully, He will make all things right in due course. In the meantime, we have a sacred responsibility to be respectful and kind to others. There is always more to their story. Always. We never know when a cruel comment will be more than someone can bear.

My travels with Sarah reminded me to:

- *Avoid the pride of comparison; it is a dead-end road.*

- *Show gratitude to the Lord for the "Bens" in my life.*

- *Be kind or be silent; most people are going through something terrible.*

QUESTIONS

Can you think of a time when someone unfairly compared you with someone else? How did it make you feel? Have you ever made unfair comparisons of others without getting all of the facts? Describe how the pride of comparison has caused you, or someone you love, emotional pain.

_____
_____
_____
_____
_____
_____

Who are the "Bens" in your life? When have you been rescued by someone sent by the Lord? Record how the rescuers in your life have helped you. Write a thank you to a "Ben" in your life.

_____
_____
_____
_____
_____
_____

How would you act differently toward others if you told yourself that most people are going through something terrible? What examples from the Savior's life demonstrate this principle?

_____
_____
_____
_____
_____
_____

Chapter Eleven

Driving Under the Influence of Pornography: Opposite Outcomes

Tammy and I met through an extended family member. She is incredibly kind on the inside and did some modeling in high school. As our friendship deepened, I learned that she ended her marriage because of her husband's pornography addiction. Tammy shared her inspiring story with me but somehow this chapter still felt unfinished. Feeling overwhelmed by the amount of marriages affected by pornography, I wondered if this addiction could be overcome. Tammy referred me to her friend, Philip, who also shared his story of triumph. With determined faith, and the enabling power of Jesus Christ's Atonement, Philip overcame a thirty-three-year addiction. Both stories are included in this chapter.

Tammy's Story in Her Own Words

I married Ethan, my returned missionary, when I was 21. From all accounts, he had served well and faithfully on his mission for the Church. At our wedding reception, all of his companions commented on what a wonderful missionary he was. I really enjoyed being married.

One Sunday, Ethan stayed home from church because he wasn't feeling well. I went across the street and attended our nearby sacrament meeting. The Holy Ghost was very strong in that particular service. When I left the chapel I was filled with the Spirit and ran home between meetings to check on my husband.

When I opened the door to our apartment, I felt a sudden darkness that was quite opposite from the beautiful Spirit I'd felt at church. As I walked down the hall by our bedroom, I noticed a pornographic magazine on the floor. My heart sank.

The dark feeling was awful. I went into the room and asked my husband about the magazine. He told me that a friend had put it in his backpack at school as a joke and admitted that he'd been tempted to look at it. Our new marriage was important to me, and I was concerned. He said he was sorry and he seemed sincere. I soon forgave him, believing that the magazine was just a one-time mistake, and it would never happen again.

Two years into our marriage, we had our first baby. Ethan worked nights and got home at two o'clock in the morning. One night I woke up at three a.m. and went into the living room. I saw Ethan sitting in front of the TV and he quickly turned it off. I asked him what he was watching—no response. I walked over and ejected the movie. My heart sank when I saw it was porn. He admitted that he'd been addicted to pornography for almost ten years. I was stunned.

Ethan finally told me about his past. At age 12, he found a stack of pornographic magazines in a field. He was tempted to look at them and hid them under his bed. That was the beginning of his addiction. He said the Holy Ghost warned him repeatedly to stop, but he didn't listen. Ethan tried to stop several times, going weeks or months without viewing, but he always crashed. He lost his confidence to change. He also struggled with the problem on his mission.

I didn't know how spiritually destructive pornography addiction was—I was naive. When I suggested counseling, Ethan refused. His addiction was much more serious than I realized.

Over the next year, I often asked how he was doing. I invited him to talk to me whenever he got the urge to view pornography and offered to help him be strong. He promised to be honest. But whenever I brought up the subject, his response was always the same. He looked me right in the eye and said, "I'm doing fine and I don't think I'll ever have a problem again."

Eight months later, I discovered what an awful hold this addiction had on him. One night, late after work, Ethan was asleep in the bedroom and I was in the living room rocking our baby. I decided to look in the front zipper pocket of his backpack. A container of tobacco lay inside.

For over a year I had been working hard to trust Ethan. I couldn't believe it. This was another shocking and painful surprise. Who was I married to? I had a feeling to call the video store to see what movies had been rented. When I called, I was told that they were all porn.

After so many lies, I felt like I'd been living with a stranger. I decided to leave him for a week to sort things out. I took our one-year-old daughter and moved in with my parents, but returned to the apartment the same night to pick up some items I'd forgotten. When I walked in, my husband was sitting on the couch watching a pornographic movie. Instead of feeling sorrow that his wife and baby had left, he was relieved that he didn't have to hide his addiction.

Ethan refused to get help or receive counseling. Through powerful experiences, I was shown that he had lost the ability to love. His heart was stone cold. I discovered that not only had he lied about his pornography and tobacco use, but that he had also been unfaithful to me. When I found out about his infidelity, he displayed no emotion. He didn't shed a single tear.

Because of the severity of his addiction, our marriage didn't have a happy ending. When I prayed, the answer for me was very clear—I was not to stay in the marriage. I felt the Lord guiding me through this experience. He led me by the hand, preparing me for the future. Because I had been living a worthy life, I felt that the Lord no longer wanted me to be deceived.

At one point during our separation, I learned about how pornography desensitizes the spirit and erodes the conscience. When my husband was viewing pornography, there was a dark feeling in our home that was thick and stifling.

Since this experience, I have researched pornography addiction. I learned that an addict loses the capacity to love and replaces that ability with lust. The addict is unable to respect their companion as a son or daughter of God. Instead, the partner is turned into an object. The lust is short-lived, so the addict quickly tires of his partner and starts looking for someone new and exciting. The spouse becomes the drug. Once the drug wears off, they move on to someone else.

Men and women need to ask questions about pornography use before marriage. Don't be afraid to ask someone you're dating what their experiences are with pornography. Find out if they have ever had an addiction. If asking these questions makes them uncomfortable, you may already have your answer. You want a man or woman that will be capable of loving you always.

For married couples, this addiction needs to be addressed often. We live in a pornographic society and must have regular and open dialogue with our spouses. Discussing how both partners are combating this temptation can be a powerful reminder for us to be on guard. We need to put safety nets in place to prevent exposure. Never allow a spouse to bring pornography into a relationship with the claim that it will enhance your love life. This is a lie.

Pornography will kill the love and replace it with lust.

It's important to educate ourselves and our children about pornography addiction. Teach them how destructive this addiction is. When someone is viewing porn, the Spirit immediately withdraws. Help them learn how it destroys the ability to have a loving and lasting relationship.

This is only one story about pornography addiction. The decision to leave a marriage is between you and God. He is the only one who can look into the heart of a man or woman. When you stay close to God, He will guide you and carry you down the path you should take.

When someone has chosen to become continually involved in pornography, they are driving through much of their lives under the influence of Satan. The Lord's light is always there, ready to drive the darkness away. Lasting peace can only be obtained by inviting our Savior to do what only He can do—save us.

Philip Harrison overcame a thirty-three year pornography addiction. I read his book and his experiences helped educate me about addiction. He has not relapsed for many years and has been determined to educate others. I connected Sheri with Philip, who agreed to share his story.

Philip's Story in His Own Words

I cannot take any credit for overcoming my addiction. It's not me that has done this—I'm living proof that the Savior can do for us what we cannot do for ourselves. I wake up every morning and give my addiction to the Lord; He has become my best friend.

As a young teenager in the 1960s, I grew up in Provo, Utah, in an active Latter-day Saint family. I was exposed to pornography from magazines and books. It wasn't as readily available back then as it is today. Before my mission, I interviewed with my bishop and stake president, and the topic of porn never came up. There wasn't nearly the emphasis on pornography as there is now. No one ever said that if you struggled with it, you needed to talk to your bishop.

While on my mission, I attended a district conference. The district leader said that if anyone had a problem with masturbation they should talk to the mission president about it. I talked with him. He simply said, "Don't do it anymore." I struggled off and on. Back then, there wasn't much understanding regarding pornography addiction and recovery.

My girlfriend, Kathy, waited for me while I was on my mission. We were married shortly after my return. After we married, I didn't think I'd have a problem with porn, yet just a few months later, I was back into it. For several years I kept it secret from my wife. There were times I would break free from it for a few weeks or months. I had several turning points that could have been a wakeup call if I would have chosen to recover.

Throughout my struggle with addiction, I never stopped being active in the Church. I served in church callings and was an Elders Quorum president in three different States. I taught gospel doctrine and family relations classes. Over the years, my wife caught me once or twice looking at a movie with nudity. She didn't know how bad it was and the issue was glossed over.

My wife had a heart condition and had open-heart surgery twice. In spite of her health problems, we were blessed with five children. Because of her medical challenges, she was on medication that made her sleepy. One night, we were watching a movie. After she fell asleep, I turned it off and switched it to one with nudity. Kathy woke up at the right moment and asked me what I was viewing. She didn't get on my case but she was very concerned.

Kathy also struggled with a food addiction. She had been going to a twelve-step program called Overeaters Anonymous where she learned about a book, *He Did Deliver Me from Bondage*. It was written for Latter-day Saint men and women, and explained the twelve steps of overcoming addiction.

Upon reading the "About the Author" page in the back of the book, Kathy realized that the author of the book, a single woman named Colleen Bernhard, was attending Utah State University and lived just ten miles from us. My wife went to see Colleen and began attending the support group she held in her home each week. Kathy started reading the literature and I became interested in what she was reading. Through study, I was convinced that my problem with pornography was also an addiction. After Kathy had attended the group a couple of times, I asked her if we could attend together. She said sure, but wondered why I wanted to go.

When I finally admitted my addiction to her she was sobered, quiet, and concerned. She said, "Okay, let's go." The organization is called Heart t' Heart (heart-t-heart.org) and is for men and women with any addiction. It's not an official Church program, but is based on Latter-day Saint beliefs.

After twenty-eight years of marriage, I could feel a real diminishing of my spirituality. The adversary was gaining greater control over my mind. In the beginning, I could say no. But as time went by, I lost more and more of my agency. If the temptation was there, I would give in.

Ultimately, I realized that I could not handle the problem by myself and so I owned my addiction. I sensed that this twelve step support group that correlated the steps with the teachings of the restored Gospel could help me. For years, I thought I just needed more time and to try harder. Eventually, I couldn't try any harder. I felt hopeless.

Kathy and I began to attend the meetings. We used the twelve steps to deal with our individual addictions. It took time, but I was finally ready to confront my own issues. It was a process of taking the steps of repentance and breaking them down, a sort of "Repentance for Dummies." It was a much more thorough process than most people go through when they repent.

One of my first challenges was accepting how much of an addict I was. I didn't think I was as bad as an alcoholic or drug addict and my pride got in the way. The program was centered on ego reduction and humbling yourself. Each exercise was a process of deepening humility.

Kathy and I both read *He Did Deliver Me from Bondage* on our own and answered the questions at the end of every chapter. We were counseled to write out our responses so we could be thorough in our efforts, but in my pride, I didn't think I needed to take the time and wouldn't write anything down. Addicts have a tremendous problem with pride. After I got through the book, though, I found I was still struggling with overwhelming temptations to act out. Finally, I realized I had to go through each step and write out my totally honest responses to each prompt.

The unavoidable truth is you get out of these programs what you put into them. Success is based on how willing you are to be humble. Eventually, I started becoming more serious about recovery. As Kathy and I attended the support group meetings, we became close friends with Colleen and hoped to join her in administering the Heart t' Heart organization (which was the forerunner of the current Church's Addiction Recovery Program). Sadly, five months after we started going to Heart t' Heart meetings, Kathy passed away. Her heart stopped and went into ventricular fibrillation. It was a terrible time. I didn't know if my own heart would recover.

Shortly after my wife died, I had experiences with the Holy Ghost that let me know that Colleen and I were to be married.

We both had a strong confirmation of the Spirit and married five months later. We have a combined family of 17 kids.

After I married Colleen, I still had a few more slips with pornography. I continued going to meetings, working the steps and the program. A year into the program, I had my last slip. A year and eight months after I began the program, I was completely recovered. I started a Heart t' Heart program in Logan, Utah, that was for men dealing with sexual addiction issues.

For a lot of years, I thought, *I just have this problem; other than that I'm a pretty good guy.* When you start giving your soul to the devil, you don't get to say how far he will take you.

Anyone with an addiction must get help to overcome it. The Church's addiction program is based on the twelve-step program used by Alcoholics Anonymous. Many men and bishops are now becoming educated and realizing that getting married will not solve the problem. The reason that getting married doesn't help is the addiction to pornography is not about sex. It's about an addictive experience. It's an addiction to certain brain chemicals. Pornography creates and reinforces specific pathways in the brain.

What an addict lacks is power to change. They've lost the ability to say no. Many of the talks I've heard on pornography say that it's bad; don't do it. For most people, they need to know how to quit. I wrote a book called, *Clean Hands Pure Heart*, about overcoming addiction to pornography through the redeeming power of Jesus Christ. It teaches you how to get out of the addiction.

The most important part of healing is how recovery works. The addict needs to develop a relationship with the Savior. The reason I'm porn free today is because I daily give my addiction to Jesus Christ and surrender my life to Him as much as possible. The more I surrender, the more I am free. I had prayed, fasted, and tried a lot of other things. But I could not do it on my own.

The Savior has to become your best friend. You have to talk to Him. Surrender every temptation to Him; walk through your day with Him. This is part of accepting the Atonement of Jesus Christ. Have faith and act on that belief as you get to know Him. You won't develop a relationship with someone unless you talk to them. Addiction can be a tremendous blessing in a person's life if they will let it be.

Addiction will teach them their need for God.

Colleen taught me a process called "capturing" that has changed my life. This process is explained in her book, *He Did Deliver Me from Bondage*:

Capturing:

"What does "capture" mean? It means to get hold of something, and make it your own. Here's how you capture thoughts from any source:

1. Underline the words or phrases that stand out to you. If it's in the form of a lecture, take notes as you listen.
2. Get a notebook (maybe a journal) and a pen and then rewrite the words, phrases, sentences or whatever you underlined or noted from the source.
3. Now write all that comes into your mind about the thought or quote that you have previously copied into your notebook. Why was it important to you? How did it connect for you? What does it say to you? How does it apply to your life?

For me, this process of capturing thoughts, scriptures, and quotes, has also become a way of praying. I often find that I have naturally entered into a prayer mode somewhere during this process, writing prayerful thoughts, expressing myself directly to God. I nearly always find myself realizing that what I am hearing in my thoughts is the voice of the Lord, through the Holy Spirit's mediation, speaking to my mind and heart.

As you record the thoughts and impressions that come to you, you can actually read a personal conversation you are having with our Savior Jesus Christ." (Colleen C. Harrison, *He Did Deliver Me from Bondage,* Hyrum, Utah: Windhaven Publishing, 2012, p. A-3 & 4.)

Mile Marker Eleven: The Lord's Light Drives Darkness Away

Carpooling with Tammy and Philip gave me more understanding for those struggling with addiction. Tammy remained worthy and supported Ethan as he faced his addiction. Ethan made some efforts to repent, but lacked the commitment to change. Eventually, his heart was past feeling. Tammy had prepared herself to be sensitive to the *absence* of the Spirit, and received a witness from the Holy Ghost to divorce.

When Philip was ready to immerse himself in a diligent study of the scriptures, with a desire to walk with the Lord, he overcame a thirty year pornography addiction. His determination to overcome his addiction and share his journey with others is inspiring.

Our latter-day prophet, Russell M. Nelson, made an extraordinary prophetic promise to those struggling with addiction:

"My dear brothers and sisters, I promise that as you prayerfully study *The Book of Mormon* every day, you will make better decisions—every day. I promise that as you ponder what you study, the windows of heaven will open, and you will receive answers to your own questions and direction for your own life. I promise that as you daily immerse yourself in *The Book of Mormon*, you can be immunized against the evils of the day, even the gripping plague of pornography and other mind-numbing addictions." (Russell M. Nelson, "*The Book of Mormon*: What would Your Life Be Like Without It?" *Ensign*, November 2017)

Our living prophet understands our struggles. He has promised us that if we immerse ourselves in *The Book of Mormon* every day, we have the assurance that we will make better decisions every day. Then comes the extraordinary promise: *we will be immunized from mind-numbing addictions.* A prophet of God on earth today is offering us a way to be immunized from pornography and other addictions—when we do our part. This landmark promise is incredible.

My travels with Tammy and Philip taught me how important it is to:

- *Give addictive tendencies and addictions to the Lord each day.*

- *Prayerfully read and ponder The Book of Mormon daily to qualify for prophetic promises.*

- *Capture Spirit-led conversations with the Lord on paper.*

Questions

Addictions come in many forms. If you have addictions, or addictive tendencies you struggle with, are you willing to surrender them to the Lord? Why or why not? What's holding you back?

_____
_____
_____
_____
_____
_____

President Russell M. Nelson promises that if we prayerfully read and ponder The Book of Mormon daily, we will make better decisions and be immunized against pornography and other mind numbing addictions. How do you feel about this promise?

_____
_____
_____
_____
_____
_____

Recording your impressions when reading scriptures can capture a Spirit led conversation with the Lord. How do you feel knowing you can communicate with Jesus Christ on such an intimate level?

_____
_____
_____
_____
_____
_____

Chapter Twelve

Turning on the Headlights of Hope: Auguste's Faith

My great-grandmother, Auguste Dietz, survived a devastating divorce in the early 1900s. During that time, divorce was rare and considered shameful. Feeling a need to connect with Auguste, I added her to my carpool of friends. I read family histories and spoke with relatives who knew her and took poetic license in making her story come to light. During a dark time when I had lost hope, her example of faith became my beacon of light. I learned how Auguste had allowed the light of Christ to guide her to the restored Gospel of Jesus Christ, choosing a difficult path that led toward peace. This feisty German woman who was sold to her first husband, and betrayed by her second, never gave up hope.

The Story of My Great-Grandmother, Auguste Dietz

Auguste was the third child born to a family of eleven in 1868. She was raised in East Prussia, which later became Poland. Her Father was a gamekeeper of a royal estate. He was in charge of hunting to provide meat for the wealthy royals. He was considered to be a higher-ranking servant, so his family had their own cottage, though it was still primitive by our standards. He was poor and built all of his children's shoes out of wood.

The royals had a private school for their servant's children. This was very forward thinking in those days. The teachers were harsh and showed no tolerance or love. Auguste learned to read and write in German. Her sister, Johanna, was beaten so severely by the school master that she eventually died.

There was no such thing as freedom of religion. The views of the day taught about a God of vengeance. If you misbehaved or fell asleep during a church meeting, one of the deacons would walk along the aisle and the guilty person would be whipped. Auguste hated going to church, but did not have a choice. Others had portrayed God as being merciless and vengeful. She didn't understand God, but believed in her heart that Heavenly Father was kind and loving.

In Prussia, during the late 1870s, young girls were commonly sold by their families to men wanting pretty young wives. At age 16, Auguste was sold to Mr. Kling, a wealthy and much older man studying to be a doctor. This was a forced marriage of convenience for everyone except Auguste.

As a child bride, she was naïve and did not know what would be expected of her. She did not love her future husband and owner, but had no choice but to go through with the wedding. Deciding to make the best of it, she tried to be positive and accept her lot. Auguste was given her first pair of new shoes as a wedding gift, along with some other material possessions she had been deprived of as a child.

Right away, Auguste became pregnant with twin girls, Johanna and Lina. The babies were born healthy, but Johanna contracted measles shortly after birth and died three months later. This was a devastating loss. When their surviving twin, Lina, was nine months old, she contracted cholera from Auguste's husband. Tragically, both died.

Within nine months, Auguste had lost her husband and both babies. Auguste's anguish was unbearable. Karl, her older brother, was compassionate and paid for her to go to school and study nutrition. Grateful to him for his kindness, and the opportunity to focus on something besides her grief, she decided to enroll in college. When she graduated, she had hope for a better life and moved to Germany. She got a job as a nutritionist in the largest hospital in Hamburg.

While at work, Auguste met a young woman who also worked in the hospital named Lina Pope. She was five-foot-eight with flaming red hair. Auguste was four-foot-eleven, with chestnut-brown hair. They were quite a pair and became kindred spirits. It was special having another Lina in her life, the same name as one of her deceased twin daughters. In time, they got to know each other and eventually shared an apartment together. Their friendship was a rare blessing from the Lord, and they stayed in touch all of their lives.

Auguste didn't go to church, but she prayed and in her heart was a religious woman. One night, as she was walking home from work, she saw some missionaries from The Church of Jesus Christ of Latter-day Saints having a street meeting. The Spirit touched her and told her, "They are speaking the truth." As they sang, she went over to listen. She and Lina inquired about their message and were taught the Gospel of Jesus Christ. Through prayer, they both received a witness from God that the Church was true. Both were baptized and received the gift of the Holy Ghost through the power of the priesthood.

Finally, Auguste had found a religion that taught about a God of love and a merciful Savior. Losing her husband and twins to death had broken her heart, but the restored Gospel had revealed truths about eternal families. Her new beliefs gave her the knowledge and comfort that they would be reunited in the next life. To her dying day, she knew the names of the missionaries who taught her the Gospel and had given her the blessing of hope.

Throughout her life, Auguste had been guided by the light of Christ. When she chose to be baptized, she qualified for an even greater light—the Holy Ghost. This precious gift strengthened her faith.

Auguste's entire family thought she was fanatical for joining the Church. She was harassed by them for her beliefs. The persecution became so severe that she knew she would eventually have to leave the country. Together, Auguste and Lina decided to seek religious freedom. In faith, they set aside all of their extra money, saving for boat passage to the United States. After two years, the persecution became so great, they were determined to board the next boat to America.

Several days before the ship left, Auguste received word that her brother, Karl, would be at the boat to have her arrested. He wanted her committed to an insane asylum for joining the Church. The same brother who had supported her in college, and shown compassion after the death of her husband and children, had turned against her. Auguste was devastated.

In those days, women were not allowed to travel alone without a man. Desperate, the women turned to the missionaries who had baptized them and together they came up with a plan. Auguste and Lina would disguise themselves as men. The Elders gave them their suits and hats to wear so they wouldn't be recognized.

Clinging to each other and their faith, the women approached the dock and waited in line. After saving all they could for two years, they discovered they only had enough money for one of them to board the ship with a little change. Horrified, they vowed that they would go together. With every ounce of faith they possessed, the women prayed for God's intervention. Auguste was first in line, clutching their precious money, when she concocted a plan. She would give the captain enough passage for her, then discreetly pass the rest of the money to Lina, and pray the captain wouldn't notice there wasn't enough for her additional passage.

Auguste turned her head and stopped breathing. Her brother, Karl, and the constable were standing directly beside her. Both men looked frantic and angry. Karl looked right at her and she made no expression. Their eyes locked and he searched her face for several seconds. Miraculously, he turned away and continued his hunt. Auguste's heart felt like it was pounding out of her chest. When he was safely out of sight, she began to breathe. A swirling mixture of relief as well as deep sadness settled over her, sensing she would never see her brother again.

As Auguste regained her composure, she kept her eyes on the person in front of her. Determined that she and Lina were going together, she began praying with a panicked fervor. When her turn arrived, she tentatively showed the captain her money. He was about to take it from her hand and then became distracted. To her amazement he didn't collect the passage. Auguste quickly passed the money back to Lina and then quickly stepped onto the ship, making it possible for both of them to board.

Miraculously, their trick went undetected and they boarded safely. Indescribable relief swept over their quivering bodies. They had done everything in their power to save their money and escape religious persecution. At the last moment, when their situation seemed hopeless, the Lord provided multiple distractions and many miracles so they could board the ship together. Auguste and Lina knew beyond any doubt that God had answered their prayers and had a hand in their destiny. They knelt and said a sincere prayer of gratitude as they began their journey.

After many grueling weeks, the ship landed in America. Auguste came through Ellis Island and her name is engraved on the "Wall of Fame." Although she suffered the overwhelming loss of her twins and husband, and had been abandoned and betrayed by her family, she had found a new faith in the Gospel of Jesus Christ. She had hope for a better life.

As a young widow in her early thirties, Auguste wanted more children and a family. She was proud to be an American and took the train to Salt Lake City to be with the Saints. She never had the desire to return to her homeland.

Auguste became the cook for a wealthy family who owned the Bamberger Railway. Their sixteen-year-old son loved her cookies and struck her a deal; keep the cookies coming and he would teach her English. Determined to be fluent and fit into American culture, Auguste took night classes to learn the language.

A year later, she met a fellow German widower, Konrad Dietz, who had joined the Church in Germany. He had also come to the States for religious reasons. Their relationship progressed and they fell in love. Soon they were engaged with the hope of a fresh start.

When Auguste married the second time, she was 34 and Konrad was 31. They were married in the Salt Lake Temple, and she became a stepmother to six-year-old Paula and two-year-old Adolph. Over the next ten years, she gave birth to four more children. She had Henry and Alpha in her late thirties. Twenty-seven years after the passing of her first set of twins, Auguste was compensated for their death. At age 44, she gave birth to another set of twin girls, Marie and Martha.

During the early years of marriage, Konrad often got drunk and Auguste tried to hide the secret. As a professional tailor, he was a well-dressed gentleman of the times. His job was to design and create suits for wealthy men in Salt Lake City.

At age 45, Konrad became sick with kidney disease. He called upon the Elders to give him a priesthood blessing and was miraculously healed. Konrad felt the Spirit strongly and became active in the Church. Soon after, he was called on a three-year mission to Germany and was asked to go with twelve older men from Salt Lake City. Young men weren't called on missions in those days because they were serving as soldiers in World War I.

Times were hard and Auguste carried on by herself. She longed for Konrad's return so they could continue raising their family together in the Gospel. Even though he struggled with weaknesses, she believed in him and chose to find hope in their eternal family.

Konrad struggled with disobedience on his mission. One of the men he served with died and he was asked to leave his mission and accompany the body home. He traveled to America by boat with many of the immigrating converts. In spite of the circumstances, Auguste was grateful to have him home again; she was weary from raising the children alone.

When Konrad arrived, he had a young woman in her twenties with him named Gretel. She had joined the Church and needed a place to stay until she was settled. Auguste welcomed her into their home and she was treated as a member of the family. Together, they did household chores and cared for the children.

Auguste's daughter, Marie, was sharing her room with Gretel and they slept in the same bed. Over the next few months, Gretel became good friends with Auguste, Konrad, and their family. One night, Konrad came into Marie's room. He climbed into bed next to Gretel and was intimate with her. Mortified, Marie pretended to be asleep. Too petrified to move, she lay awake all night, trying to deal with the horror of her father committing adultery in her bed.

When the sun finally came up, Marie told her mother. Auguste knew in her heart that Marie was telling the truth. She confronted her husband and he didn't deny the accusation. She promptly packed up Konrad and his mistress, put their suitcases on the front porch, and demanded they leave immediately. The shock and heartbreak of her husband having an affair with another woman living in her own home was surreal—unthinkable.

When Konrad left the house, his heart was filled with swirling emotions. As he and Gretel walked down the street, Konrad stopped and visited with Brother Nelson, a neighbor who was a close friend of the family. He asked him to please do what he could to help take care of Auguste.

In those days, a divorce could only be obtained by proof of infidelity. Auguste was heartbroken watching her eleven-year-old daughter, Marie, testify against her own father. This was shameful for the family and devastating to Marie. Konrad had broken the hearts of his wife and children and a divorce was granted. Auguste was so bitter and hurt by her divorce that she was never interested in another marriage.

Auguste became a single mother at age 54. Marie and Martha were 11, Alpha was 15, and Henry was 18. Her stepchildren were young adults, Adolph was 20, and Paula was 24.

Because of economic scarcity during the Depression, most jobs were reserved for the men. Auguste was blessed to work for wealthy people in the Salt Lake Valley doing house cleaning, cooking, and anything she could find. Konrad offered to pay child support, but Auguste was too stubborn to accept it.

Auguste became head cook in the Salt Lake Temple, a paid position. Because of her employment, she had the compensatory blessing of being in the temple almost every day. When James E. Talmage, one of the twelve apostles, was commissioned to write *Jesus the Christ*, he was asked to do his writing and research in the Salt Lake Temple. Auguste had the special privilege of serving him his food. Spending time in the temple with prophets and apostles strengthened her as a single mother.

Auguste's daughter, Alpha, my paternal grandmother, dropped out of school in the eighth grade to help support the family. Later, during the Depression, she served a mission in the Eastern United States. Auguste was a hard worker and determined to be self-reliant. Even during the Depression, she was miraculously blessed with the means to provide support to Alpha on her mission and sustain herself and her children.

Auguste had a cheery personality and loved to laugh. She was surrounded by friends and family throughout her life. In spite of fierce opposition, she loved the Lord and was compensated in many ways. Her bishop respected her and little was ever said about her broken marriage. It would have been considered cruel in those days to refer to her divorce. Instead, she was treated kindly as a widow, from tragically losing her first husband to cholera.

The latter–day prophet, Joseph F. Smith, and his wife, Jessie Evans Smith, were close personal friends to Auguste. President Smith stayed in touch with her throughout her older years. When she passed away, the prophet honored her by speaking at her funeral. His wife sang in her beautiful contralto voice, *"The King of Glory."*

Auguste was a survivor of divorce and a true follower of Christ. She left her extended family, culture, and country for her beliefs—and she never gave up hope.

Mile Marker Twelve: Turn on the Headlights of Hope

When I became acquainted with Auguste's story through family history, I was struggling to find hope. For a time, putting the words divorce and hope in the same sentence made me want to scream. I had always believed that God wouldn't give me more than I could handle—until my marriage ended. It felt impossible to actually live through so much chronic heartbreak.

While navigating my divorce, I couldn't see light at the end of the tunnel. I didn't know how to keep going day after day; the depression was debilitating. It felt like darkness would envelop me forever. I didn't know how to love myself and did very little self-care. When I look back at that time through the rear-view mirror, I see how I was carried beyond my own capacity.

Eventually, I learned that when we're traveling through dark tunnels of despair, the Savior's light is the high beam that guides our way. His light fueled my journey through the dark tunnel, empowering me to face the darkness head on; something I could not do on my own. With Him, I was enough. Without Him, forget it.

Hope is the beam of light rising above the horizon of our present circumstances.

Divorce survivors are pioneers traveling through uncharted territory with no paved roads. After natural disasters, people all over the world rise up through the ashes of adversity and begin again. Communities share a common purpose as they rebuild, re-create, and restore their lives together. Cities are reconstructed, taking on a new shape and personality. Stronger foundations are poured and homes are rebuilt. Similar to divorce, new roads are paved and yet they look different from the old.

When facing an impasse, God, in His infinite wisdom, decides whether to move the mountain or help us climb—it's up to Him. But rest assured, He will be our guiding light. Through our Savior, hope and help is available to all—even the betrayer. I find comfort knowing that the peace of Jesus Christ's Atonement is meant for both of my great-grandparents and for me.

My great-grandmother Auguste taught me:

- *With the Lord's help, I will be given strength to climb the mountains in front of me.*

- *To feel the light of hope we must learn to love and care about ourselves.*

- *If Auguste could lose everything and rebuild again; I could too.*

Questions

What mountains have you faced from your own divorce or the divorce of someone close to you? Has the Lord removed your mountains? What mountains remain? Can you identify specific ways Heavenly Father has helped you climb?

_____
_____
_____
_____
_____

We are commanded to love ourselves as much as others. If God gave you a report card on the subjects of self-love and self-care, what grades do you think you would receive? Why?

_____
_____
_____
_____
_____

What material things did you or someone you care about lose in divorce? Are you still holding onto those things mentally? Why or why not? How has divorce changed your view of material things? If you lost possessions, money, or good credit, how is God helping you rebuild?

_____
_____
_____
_____
_____

Chapter Thirteen

Unloading the Junk in the Trunk: Shannon's Awakening

I met Shannon at a Cub Scout activity and our sons became friends. She was an enthusiastic Scout leader with an enormous smile and a sassy haircut. Shannon was a strong and capable single mother of three young children. Her energy blew me away. Eagerly, I invited her to join my carpool. God placed Shannon on my path when I felt stranded from lugging around emotional junk. Exhausted from the weight, I needed help letting it go. Shannon had worked hard to release her emotions from the past and move forward. When she told me she had thrown dishes in the dumpster, it was all over—I had to know more.

Shannon's story in her own words

After four years of marriage, my husband, Dan, sent me to Utah to meet with his psychiatrist and counselor. According to him, this was the only way our marriage could be saved. I knew I was struggling with depression, so I believed him. Our family lived in Montana, so logistically this was difficult. The kids and I would live with extended family and we would be apart for several months while I went to counseling.

We had a one-year-old, a two-year-old, and I was four months pregnant. My third pregnancy was unplanned and I was not happy. We were reeling from a recent job loss just weeks after we had finished building a new home. Dan and I were having money problems and the financial pressure was mounting.

Something was forcing me against my will to move through a very difficult situation.

I felt like I had climbed up to the top of a slide and was getting ready to fly down, but I was being pushed when I wasn't ready to go. Feeling powerless to hold on, I felt like I was being thrust to the bottom.

Once in Utah, I met Dan's therapist. I explained to him that in spite of the current circumstances, Dan and I had everything going for us. We were both returned missionaries, had gotten married in the temple, and had two beautiful children with one on the way. After the second visit, he reassured me that I was just fine, and anyone in my circumstances would have anxiety. The therapist said I was a really nice lady and I thought, *gosh, I'll pay you another hundred and twenty dollars.*

While I was receiving therapy, my husband traded his family life for a social life. He had undergone gastric bypass surgery the year before and when he lost weight, his personality changed. Even though he was shedding pounds, he still had addictive tendencies. Instead of replacing his food addiction with something positive, he traded it for alcohol, gambling, and girls.

After several months, Dan came to Utah to be with us during the holidays. On Christmas night, he brought up divorce. I was pregnant and divorce was out of the question—I was completely in denial. He left us with family in Utah and returned to Montana, even though I was almost ready to deliver our third child.

The day I went into labor I knew something was very wrong in my marriage. Dan said he would arrive back in Utah later that evening. Surprisingly, he arrived at the hospital before me—I had no idea he was already back in Utah. When I went to hug him, it was like hugging a cold pole. He showed absolutely no emotion.

Uncharacteristically, I wanted my whole family at the birth. I desperately needed their support because I knew I was having the baby by myself. My husband was simply taking up space and stealing air. He showed no support or love. Dan was there to do his duty because it looked good and looks were now very important to him. After the birth, he briefly held the baby and then said goodbye—he was leaving.

I had been abandoned by my husband and was totally alone.

The nurse wheeled me from the delivery room to the maternity ward, hooked me up to tubes and monitors, and left me there. I looked down as blood started gushing everywhere. Panicked, I pushed the call button but it seemed to take forever before a nurse arrived to help.

Our son, Tommy, had complications, and I was left to make decisions by myself.

The next time I saw Dan was to serve him divorce papers. The baby was only two months old and I was trying to call his bluff and give him a wake-up call. Deep down, I didn't think I would ever get divorced. We had only been married for five years. Depression consumed me and I took the responsibility of the whole marriage to heart. Inside, I still believed that all of the marital problems were my fault. I had low self-esteem and didn't believe I was good enough for my husband to be happy.

As a victim of abuse, you tend to think that you should be responsible for everything and everyone. I thought if I were a better wife then our marriage would work. Ironically, I was a great wife and neither one of us could see it. At that point in my life, I was very dependent on needing to serve others but had no clue about how to be served. To become a balanced individual, I needed to be able to accept both.

Instead of engaging in life, I was a spectator. I hadn't allowed myself to feel or express anger. When I finally gave myself permission to get mad, that's when everything shifted. Three years after we divorced, I finally went through a healing process. Until I was strong enough to handle the pain in a safe environment, my mind blocked it out. With young children, I had no concept of having any of my personal needs met. Until then, I had been in automatic mode taking care of three babies. Night after night, I would plead with God to give me four or five hours of consecutive sleep.

One day, a concerned friend ordered me to spend twenty-five dollars on new sheets. I was still sleeping on the same sheets I had when I was married. There are gouge marks in my kitchen table from the scissors I used when I began to thrash the sheets I had from my wedding. My anger started to release.

I felt absolutely nothing when I looked at the pictures from my broken marriage. I had to train myself to acknowledge my emotions and allow the anger to come at its own pace. As I gave myself permission to feel, I took my dishes and started throwing them in the dumpster in front of my apartment. Then I began yelling at them because they wouldn't break!

I finally forced myself to experience my emotions and the fury unleashed. My vision changed and I began to recognize that I was actually divorced. Until that point, I really wasn't ready to experience the emotional pain. When I finally allowed myself to feel the pain, I began to heal—spiritually, mentally, and emotionally.

The weight of my stewardship was overwhelming. I would go grocery shopping at night with three babies and angrily drive my 1973 bright green Suburban to the store. I was alone in the responsibility for our little ones and I was tired. Three car seats with a baby in each were lined up side by side in the back seat. Each week, we barely survived the shopping trip. As I unloaded the groceries, the kids, and diaper bags, I was sobbing as I thought, *I hate this.*

I learned that hating was so painful.

My negative emotions were excruciating—I didn't want to ache anymore. Finally, I decided that I was the only one that was going to do the dishes and put the babies to bed, so I had better enjoy it. I was truly blessed to finally be able to get to that point. Many people grow accustomed to the pain.

The devil wants to take us down. When we buy into Satan's whisperings, we will collapse into despair. When that happens, hope is obliterated. At that stage, there's no energy to recover or engage in life.

Divorce creates so much loss that thoughts of reengaging in life stay hidden inside a pothole of despair. At times I felt like giving up. Pulling me out of that hole literally took all of the physical, emotional, and spiritual strength I could find. In spite of doing my best to keep my family intact, my marriage was totaled beyond repair.

When addressing this kind of pain, knowing where to begin can be difficult.

Tommy, the newborn I had during my separation, was a key factor for my healing. My son had more aggressive behaviors than what I had seen before in a toddler. While I was going to college, he attended the children's preschool at the university. He had to be watched all the time around other children his age. Without provocation, he would reach out and pull their hair, scratch, or even bite them. He would attack other children in the nursery at church, at preschool, or the McDonald's Playland.

Tommy went to his first therapist at age 3. One of the teachers at his school suggested that I also work with a counselor. Tommy's problems were the miracle that helped me heal. While we were at counseling, I was introduced to an adult therapist who worked in the same office. I saw this man four to five hours a week. As he coached me in parenting and personal growth, I recognized him as one of my gifts from heaven.

As a pioneer, I am changing family patterns and there are no paved roads. I'm in the trenches. It's a lot of work, but the effort is worth it. Every pathway leads to something new, and every road we've paved makes it easier for those who come after. We are helping future generations to come. In order to move forward, I needed to have clean hands, a pure heart, and a clear head.

My children recently brought home a DVD to watch and the cover was offensive. I told them they would need to watch it somewhere else but not in my house. I am in charge of keeping my home clean and will not be intimidated by my kids. I have a favorite feather duster I pull out when they are being contentious. As I wave it around, I act like I'm cleaning up the children, reminding them to stop throwing up emotionally on each other. Their anger makes a mess of my house.

The Earth is abundant, full of all the tools we need, including counselors, scriptures, mentors, books, and the Internet. If I wanted to be healed and pass that legacy on to my children, I needed to get to work. I was in charge of my healing, no one else.

As a child, I depended on my Heavenly Father because I didn't have a father in the home. I had become very serious, living in survival mode. I was naive because I relied on the counsel of the Spirit for every minor decision. That's all I knew. The Spirit was teaching me that I didn't need to be so dependent. I finally realized that I was capable of making decisions.

I've been divorced from my ex-husband for thirteen years. For eight of those years, he was in prison for fraud. I never investigated the full reasons for his imprisonment because it wasn't worth the investment in time or emotion. It was the healthiest choice I could have made. Instead, I chose to look at the present and prepare for the future.

There's a mentality that changes from surviving to thriving. I had been afraid of prosperity. What will it be like? Will I find joy in abundant living?

Today, I am in a place that I've never been before. We live in an amazing home that is more than I ever expected. Looking back, I can see how the adversity has served me. I didn't expect to be able to support a family and live in a large home. Through faithfulness and obedience, the Lord wants us to have good things. He cares about our deepest desires, not just our needs. This has been an awakening for me.

When you wait upon the Lord, He will give you more than you ever expected or needed. And when the Lord decides to bless us, it's all rights reserved. We may not even want the blessing. When my marriage dissolved, I quit wanting things. I had been living on a needs only basis—I turned off the want gear.

When we keep God's commandments and accept the circumstances that we're in, His eternal laws say we will be blessed. Wants and blessings came to me in surprising ways. They came with a Scout leader knocking on the door after sensing the needs of my son. They came with free LEGOLAND passes from a friend. They came with the stirrings of faith in my children, who immediately bow their heads and start praying every time my car breaks down. Someone came to my house after church because he noticed a flat tire. I told him it was Sunday and he said, "Don't you need to go to work tomorrow?"

Listening to the Spirit caused me to succumb and practice following the will of God. I wanted so badly to be cleansed from the pain of my broken marriage that my heart ached. When we hold on, the light will come, although it may be years down the road. As I fostered the desire to be obedient, I didn't know I would be this blessed.

Years later, with perspective, I understand that we are each accountable to ourselves, God, and others. What we do with the accountability is where the agency steps in. Through obedience, I am entitled to have His Spirit with me and take responsibility for my healing.

In return, I can rejoice because of the peace in my heart.

Mile Marker Thirteen: Give Your Load to the Lord

When Shannon became my carpool friend, she mentored me, helping me choose to let go of the pain. Learning how to release my emotions was difficult. Holding onto emotional junk was comforting in its own way. When I clung to my emotional pain, issues began to stack. It was like trying to drive with a thousand pounds of "junk in the trunk." I needed a way to lighten the load; I was emotionally stranded. It was hard because letting go meant being vulnerable.

For a long time, I didn't know how to make peace with the pain. "Just surrender," people said. I finally learned that surrendering to God doesn't mean giving up on my righteous desires; instead, it meant learning to embrace them.

When I started to surrender my junk—I began to live.

Our Savior demonstrated the ultimate surrender of trust by being a willing captive to human agency. He knows *everything* there is to know about brutal beatings and broken hearts. With confidence, He surrendered His will to the Father's. Likewise, we too can surrender our will to His. Because of Jesus Christ's perfect love for us, He allowed His heart to literally be broken so He could carry the excruciating heartache of every divorce survivor:

"At Golgotha, He 'poured out his soul unto death' (Isaiah 53:12), and *His great heart literally broke* with an all-encompassing love for the children of God." (Bruce D. Porter, "A Broken Heart and a Contrite Spirit," *Ensign*, Nov. 2007, p. 32, emphasis added)

Not everything broken is meant to be fixed.

An important part of letting go includes assuming responsibility for our circumstances. Remember, being responsible does not mean we are accountable for another's choices. It means choosing to not hold onto a victim mentality, with the hope that our positive actions, coupled with faith and trust in our Savior, will make a difference over time.

I learned from traveling with Shannon to:

- *Let go of my emotional junk in the trunk.*
- *Surrender my emotional struggles by accepting God's will in my life.*
- *Assume responsibility for my circumstances.*

Questions

Are you holding on to any emotional junk relating to your divorce or the divorce of another? If so, is there an emotional payoff for you to keep holding on, and not let go? Pray to identify the reasons for not surrendering certain struggles. Record your impressions.

_____
_____
_____
_____
_____

How can emptying your "junk in the trunk" help you surrender certain emotional struggles? Make a list of emotional junk you want to let go of. Pray for direction and help in surrendering to God's will. Set specific goals.

_____
_____
_____
_____
_____

What difficult circumstances have you accepted regarding your divorce or the divorce of someone close to you? If applicable, write down the ways you have chosen to be responsible for your circumstances. How have these changes brought more peace into your life?

_____
_____
_____
_____
_____

Chapter Fourteen

The Precarious Path: Claire's Unthinkable Sacrifice

I met Claire while cleaning our church. She was kind, had a beautiful smile, and was incredibly hardworking. Twice a year, we met up for our cleaning assignment and scrubbed toilets together. We related to each other because of divorce and became friends. One Saturday, while mopping floors, she told me that thirty years earlier, her ex-husband had falsely accused her of sexually abusing her son. Speechless, I tried to form a response. Astonished by the courage of this woman, I wanted to learn from her experiences. Claire had struggled with depression and PTSD for most of her life. She helped me realize that because of the trauma of divorce, I, too, was severely depressed. Carpooling with Claire changed my life.

Claire's story in her own words

My mother always asked me why I wasn't "normal." As a child, I was a late bloomer and would rather be out in a field playing with horses than inside with dolls. I had a sister and an older half-brother. When I became a teenager, I had female health problems, low self-esteem, and I couldn't concentrate in school.

Mom suffered from depression and anxiety. Her form of discipline involved yelling and name calling. Sometimes I woke up in the middle of the night with her standing over my bed, yelling at me and calling me stupid. Once, my mom hired a psychic to come over and figure out what was wrong with me. This upbringing led me to believe I wasn't "normal." Mom's negative attitude made my severe depression and anxiety worse. As a child I didn't receive any medical treatment for my mental health challenges.

The Mitchell family moved next door when I was 5. They were always there for me, for all of us. Our families became best friends. They had three boys and a girl. Their mother, Carol, became my role model. She filled a huge hole in my heart by offering me love and acceptance. Secretly, I wished my mother was like her.

One of my goals as a youth was to have a horse. When I was 15, I had saved enough money to buy one. It took some doing, but Dad finally relented and let me buy Nikki. From then on, I had an escape from my mother. The only place I felt peace was with Nikki as I rode her for hours. I dated a little during my senior year, but Nikki was my biggest love. Often, I would ask both her and God, "What is wrong with me? Why does my mom think I'm stupid?"

As a teenager, I went to Bible studies full of unanswered questions. I loved puzzles and, for me, the Gospel was like a big jigsaw puzzle. But there were missing pieces.

When I was 17, I started dating my next-door childhood friend, Allen Mitchell. Right after graduation, Allen went into the service. A few months after he left, he wrote me a letter proposing marriage, but I was not ready. Shortly after my refusal, he married someone else.

While attending college in the early 1970s, I was depressed. Over the next four years, I met different men, but never felt that spark. I had so much anxiety that I would have to drink a couple of beers to calm down enough to go out on a date.

By the time I was 23, Allen had gotten divorced. As soon as I saw him again, I felt something between us. He was tall, strong, and handsome. On our first date, we drove through the country and talked for hours. Allen was a policeman, living in a town on the coast, so we wrote back and forth every day. We both loved camping and fishing and had much in common. We were in love and soon married. Our marriage further connected two close families.

After trying to get pregnant for several years, I went to a fertility doctor, and we tackled the ongoing gauntlet of tests. I still had unresolved emotional and physical issues, but I thought a family of my own would help me feel normal. Finally, I would be able to give unconditional love to my children.

During this time, Allen's uncle told us about the Church. All I knew about members of The Church of Jesus Christ of Latter-day Saints was that they were different from the other Christians I was raised with. We met with the missionaries, and after several months we were baptized. The Gospel was the missing piece; it finally made sense. I was filled with hope. A year later, Allen and I went to the temple. What a blessing to be sealed to such an amazing man. However, soon after our sealing, he became tired of going to church.

Our marriage was solid, but Allen was a type-A personality. He was strong, confident, a cop's cop, and he was becoming quite controlling. I was still trying to get pregnant and prayed for additional help. Allen began taking extended camping and fishing trips with friends and co-workers, leaving me home alone to mind the eight-acre farm. Desperately wanting to connect with my husband, I begged him to take me on outings, but he rejected my pleas.

Finally, I got pregnant but lost the baby—and almost lost my life. It was an ectopic pregnancy requiring emergency surgery, leaving me with only one functioning fallopian tube. I turned to God and received a special priesthood blessing. Inside, I still felt a flicker of hope. After I recovered, we began trying again, but it was physically painful. I decided I was done with medical treatments. In prayer, I told Heavenly Father I didn't know if I could try anymore. Six weeks later, I found out I was pregnant with our first child. We couldn't believe it.

Kyle was our miracle baby, a gift from my Heavenly Father. Two years later, another miracle happened and I became pregnant with Mandy. I was blessed with another healthy pregnancy and delivery. Now we had two beautiful babies and I finally felt like a normal person.

Allen kept taking trips, doing the things I loved to do outdoors, but always leaving me home alone to manage the farm and two small children. Over time, he emotionally detached from me. My panic attacks became common and I didn't know where to turn for help. I kept praying for guidance; I wanted to be happy and grateful for what I had. As I tried to pray away the depression, I did not understand how desperately I needed medical attention.

I felt like a piece of furniture, an inanimate object with no identity, who was only there for my husband to use. My soul longed for an emotional and physical connection with Allen. Instead, I was rejected. He claimed I was clingy and codependent. Then he withheld love, which encouraged me to become even more codependent.

When the kids were 2 and 4, Allen and I went on a trip to the coast with my parents. We went on a walk by the beach and I asked him why he didn't want to spend time with me. The conversation turned into an argument. He said, "You are stupid, worthless, and a poor excuse for a wife." The agony I felt was indescribable. I withdrew.

We went to counseling, but he simply argued, unwilling to address the issues. Finally, I reached my breaking point—I wanted a divorce. Until then, that word had never entered my mind. I had been committed to the marriage, regardless. Because of low self-esteem, I didn't know I had the right to stand up to him or to set healthy boundaries for myself.

Several weeks later, I took the kids to the coast for an overnight outing. When I returned home, I discovered Allen had moved out and begun dating a friend's co-worker named Susan. A few days later, we talked and I hoped that maybe we could work things out. Deep down I didn't want a divorce—I loved my husband. However, within two weeks, Allen and Susan moved in together. They married as soon as the divorce finalized.

I lost it.

With no time to prepare for such sudden changes, I had suicidal thoughts and was in shock. When you're depressed you block things out because of the pain. My sister intervened, suggesting professional help. We both knew I needed intensive counseling to get to the root of my problems, so I spent ten days at a mental health facility. I realized I couldn't pray my depression away, but prayer helped me deal with it. Finally, I got on some medications that helped me calm down and think better.

Going to church and seeing intact families was emotionally painful. Even though I believed I was a child of God, I didn't think even He could find me worthwhile. It was a struggle to be a good mom and to function, but I never abused my children.

Allen and I agreed to joint custody and the children lived with me. Every other weekend, when I dropped off the kids at their dad's, they cried, not wanting to go. It broke my heart. When they were with me, we did special things together. In counseling, I learned about healthy ways to parent. I did my best to improve.

Susan (my ex's new wife) "befriended" me and said I needed to be "up" for the kids. She claimed it was bad for them to be around me while I was depressed. She was a smooth talker and convinced me to let the kids stay with them for a time while I worked through my depression. I would still have visits every other weekend and one night a week. Slowly, I was descending into a dark hole. I didn't realize they would use my depression against me, so I agreed to the change. As soon as they had control of our children, their attitude shifted.

Allen's uncle lived with them and we had remained friends. He told me about Allen and Susan's parental alienation tactics to brainwash our kids. Kyle and Mandy would ask me to attend their special events and Allen refused to give me the information. Other times, he would lie to me about where the kid's activities were. Susan would tell the children I didn't love them. As part of the brainwashing, she told the kids I was picking them up when a visit wasn't arranged. This shattered their trust in me.

Eventually, Kyle wouldn't come with me. Sometimes it was his choice, other times he was grounded. I loved my children, and had done the best I could, but I was being rejected by my son. My heart was broken.

Susan was well-educated in child sexual abuse and occult studies. She worked at a major university as a professor and eventually became a cultist herself. She was considered an expert in the community in recognizing sexual abuse in children and was frequently called into the courts as an expert witness. Susan secretly put the children in counseling with an unethical professional who later lost her license for being inappropriate with children.

I could feel my kids drifting and did all I could to preserve our relationship. My therapist and I had a meeting with Allen, Susan, and the kids' counselor. The attitude of their counselor was shocking. They were trying to separate me from our kids by using my depression against me. One day, when I went to pick them up, God gave me a glimpse of Susan through spiritual eyes. The hair on the back of my neck stood up—I felt evil emanating from her.

A year later, my dad was hospitalized with heart disease. When he died, I was thrown into another level of depression. Immediately, Allen and Susan attacked. They said it wasn't "safe" for the kids to attend the funeral with me. I went alone, desperately needing love and support from our children. The grief was crushing.

I filled the void in my life by dating lots of men. When I met Keith, I fell hard and fast. Desperate to be loved, I married him on the rebound, hoping we'd have a good life together.

On Kyle's tenth birthday, I picked him up for our weekend visit. He was agitated and acting like a teen with raging hormones. He told me that Susan loved to run around the house naked and he really liked it. I was very disturbed and called an attorney to see if there was something I could do.

Nothing could have prepared me for what happened next.

A few days later there was a knock on the door. Two DCS workers entered my home and said, "We are not going to arrest you right now, but it could happen at any time." They claimed that my son, Kyle, had accused me of touching him inappropriately. I stood there in shock, unable to comprehend what was going on. According to them, Kyle had reported this to Susan and his counselor. I had never touched my children inappropriately—ever.

That was the last time I *ever* had contact with my children.

Immediately, I called my bishop to get help processing through the horror. As time went on, I had different attorneys, spent thousands of dollars, and paid child support for kids I could not see. I went into a spiral of darkness that took years to claw out of. My former in-laws, who were my dearest friends, were told by Allen that if they had any more contact with me he would disown them and they would never see their grandchildren again.

I lost everything. They raped my soul and stole my life. There was a hole in my being that nothing could fill. My soul ached to hear the words, "Mom, I love you" again. I cried constantly and began to know the depths of pain I never imagined a human being could endure. When I thought of Christ's suffering, I had a new understanding of His sacrifice for us. It was impossible to imagine anyone volunteering to go through so much pain and agony.

My new husband could not deal with the onslaught of accusations. Shortly after DCS had showed up at my home, we divorced. I was totally alone; it felt like God was silent.

As the court battles continued, the accusations escalated from inappropriate touching, to rape. I thought I was going to lose my mind. In order to cope with the things they accused me of and listen to them describe me as this deranged, deplorable human being, I had to emotionally step out of myself to deal with the horror.

Allen and Susan were pressuring me into giving them the children legally, including having their police friends come to my door and harass me. I received phone calls at 3 a.m. from someone threatening me. The persecution was unbearable. Susan was able to block any contact with the kids, even with supervision. My attorney in family court had experienced similar cases. He informed me that we could keep going, and spend thousands of dollars, but the children were so brainwashed that I would never get visitation rights. He also believed that the stress would kill me if I kept fighting, and he advised me to surrender my parental rights.

One particular night, I was alone and distraught. Knowing I couldn't help my son became so distressing that I could not breathe. I felt like I was dying. Silently, I cried out to God for help. All at once, I heard a voice say, "I know what is happening and they are being watched over." Finally, I turned to my Heavenly Father and found some relief.

During this time, I had people investigating Susan and the counselor. I went out of the county to another police department and presented my case. Their conclusion was the same as my attorney's. Although it wasn't fair or right, because of Allen's ties to the local police departments and Susan's clout with the courts, they recommended that I wait until the kids were older and let them make contact with me. In time, my bishop also felt the same way.

Nancy, my Relief Society president, prayed with me. Over the span of many months, we weighed the options. Finally, with many tears and much heartbreak, I signed over my parental rights to my ex-husband and his wife. I left the attorney's office a shell of a human being. There was no solace. I felt dead—I may as well have been dead.

Susan told people I had sold my kids.

I was never "formally" charged; Allen and Susan just wanted me out of their lives. Thank goodness I didn't go to prison. My son, Kyle, was completely brainwashed. He truly believed I had sexually abused him and that I didn't care about him.

My divorce was the atom bomb of divorce; a nuclear holocaust.

As I continued counseling for many years, I slowly began to recover. Wherever I moved, I contacted my bishop to let him know where I was. Seeing families with children at church was unbearable; emotionally it was too painful to attend. My feelings of hatred and resentment were eating me alive. Because of the severe PTSD resulting from being wrongfully accused, it took years for me to feel safe around children. I was jumpy and startled by the slightest thing.

At age 68, I still have much sorrow and grief, especially during the holidays, but a few years ago I overcame my feelings and surrendered them to the Lord. Finally, I felt worthy enough to enter the temple and was ready to get a recommend. It has been a cleansing balm to go to the temple and feel Heavenly Father's beautiful healing spirit. When I enter that holy place, I feel peace. I am sealed to my children and have the promise that if I stay worthy, I will be reunited with my kids. That is a goal I will never waver from.

For a time, Facebook allowed me to monitor my children and their families. I was able to access some information and pictures of my kids and grand kids. Unfortunately, I have now been blocked from that also. Today, Kyle is 37 and a single father of a young son and daughter. Mandy is 34. They are both police officers and valuable members of society. They were raised with much affluence and have traveled the world. I'm so grateful they are doing well.

From the beginning of my conversion to the Gospel, I was given some profound spiritual experiences and knew the Church was true. I held onto my faith as I slowly made my way back to the land of the living.

After intensive counseling and gaining insight into my depression, I began to understand myself. It was a profound revelation when I learned that it's okay to be different. I had to overcome much grief, bitterness, hatred, feelings of betrayal, and abandonment, before I could embrace the whole Gospel. But I always kept the Lord with me in my heart.

Fifteen years ago, I remarried. I have made many friends and become closer to my Father in Heaven. My current ward has helped me to heal. After years of trying to live without my children, I have accepted that they are in God's hands. They were His first.

I've worked hard to let go of the past, truly forgive, and heal my soul. Finally, I am at a tolerable place. I am very involved with a wonderful horse sanctuary for animals that have been abused and neglected. They give so much back to me. Once more I have a place of peace that heals my heart.

In hindsight, I would have done many things differently. I would have been more open to the Lord, relying on His help. These decisions would have given me the strength to attend church and stay stronger in the Gospel.

When battling depression, I would have been relentless about trying to figure out why I was depressed. I would have gotten counseling and medical treatment much sooner. Instead of allowing myself to believe I was stupid or abnormal, I would have loved and valued myself, honoring my unique qualities. The Lord's hand has been there helping me all along. I feel lucky that I've come out the other end as a sane person.

Yes, divorce can be ugly and treacherous, but the growth and insight I have been given has been indescribable. My Heavenly Father blessed me with the strength to eventually overcome. He opened my eyes to many lessons the Savior wants all of us to learn. Some people think their situation is hopeless and they will never recover, but they will. You can climb out of that black hole if you keep fighting and trusting in God. He is my salvation. Without that little bit of faith in Him, I would not have survived.

Mile Marker Fourteen: Recognize the Signs of Depression and Take Action

When I met Claire, I was facing custody issues. The stressors I faced after my divorce had become paralyzing. Every day I woke up with more emotional pain. I struggled to see my worth and falsely believed my kids might be better off without me. Desperate for the pain to end, my unhealthy thoughts grew. I didn't recognize the signs of depression.

As I wrote Claire's story, I recognized similar symptoms of depression within myself. I filled out a depression questionnaire and realized I had been severely depressed for over a year. I was in desperate need of medical care. Why hadn't I recognized these signs in myself?

I learned an important lesson: A troubled mind often can't think itself well.

After an assessment, the doctor prescribed an anti-depressant. This was a prayerful and personal decision. Medication is not the answer for everyone. For me, it was absolutely necessary. Because my depression was so severe, I could not feel any comfort from Heavenly Father or my Savior. I was not able to recognize that I was already safe in the arms of Their love.

With help from priesthood leaders, medication, and continued counseling, I started to think more clearly. I also began to get more rest, eat healthier, and exercise. My medication kicked in on Christmas Eve. It was as if a black curtain lifted off of my mind and I laughed for the first time in months. The relief I felt was palpable. As I laid my burdens at the feet of my Savior and accessed the power of His Atonement, the anguish finally eased.

Depression is a misunderstood illness. The stigma attached needs to be addressed so survivors will get help. There is no shame in acknowledging and treating this illness. When I began struggling with my eyesight, I needed to see an eye doctor. Wishing I could see better wasn't enough—what a relief when I got glasses. When treating mental health issues, we should turn to the Lord and, when needed, seek medical attention. Recognizing the signs of depression and getting help can save lives.

I learned from Claire that:

- *My depression was so severe I could not pray my way out of it.*
- *A troubled mind often can't think itself well.*
- *Recognizing the signs of depression and seeking help can save lives.*

QUESTIONS

What are your beliefs about depression? After reading about Claire and learning about my experiences, did your beliefs about depression change? If so, describe your thought process.

_____
_____
_____
_____
_____
_____

If depression is affecting you or your loved ones, what steps have you taken to address this illness? Pray for inspiration regarding your situation and courage to act. Create a plan.

_____
_____
_____
_____
_____
_____

What support systems do you have in place for yourself and/or family? As additional support, if you live in the US, keep the national crisis hot line number available for yourself, loved ones, and children: 1-800-273-8255. The crisis text line is: 741741. Text the word "HOME" in the message bar. The number connects you with a crisis worker in your area.

_____
_____
_____
_____
_____
_____

Chapter Fifteen

A Fork in the Road: My Test

Over time, I came closer to a place of acceptance regarding divorce. When I welcomed help from members of my carpool, most importantly my Heavenly Father and Jesus Christ, I felt more peace. As I focused on being a mother, I became more fully aware of my children's needs and decided to spend the rest of my life dedicated to them. I had no desire to date or remarry—ever. Being hit on by strange men was unnerving; I didn't know how to handle awkward situations. I also wanted to set good boundaries for myself and be kind. When I called my sister Janna for advice, she said I needed classes. *What in the world? Dating classes?*

The Dating Workshop

Janna had seven years of experience as an older single adult. She told me I needed classes from Utah's "dating coach," Alisa Goodwin Snell. *Seriously?* I had never heard of such a thing. The classes taught singles about many aspects of dating, including how to handle awkward situations when you weren't ready to date. I took my sister's advice and did a Google search. The instructor was giving a free dating workshop in a couple of weeks close to my area. With nothing to lose, I signed up, determined to learn the basics of avoiding men.

Shortly after, an unexpected health crisis hit our family and one of my children was very ill. Facing this emergency alone was daunting. My peace flew out the window and I was sinking. It's interesting how you can feel like you've made progress in healing from your divorce and then a crisis hits and your emotions begin to unravel.

Many hurtful memories I had experienced in relation to divorce came back to torture me tenfold. It felt like all of the emotional work I had done to move forward had never happened.

I was at a low point.

My parents were serving a two year mission in England, and I missed them terribly. I desperately wanted a priesthood blessing from my father. Fortunately, I had others I could turn to. My close friends, James and Cheri, were a great support to me and were aware of my circumstances. James graciously agreed to give me a blessing.

When he laid his hands on my head, I immediately felt peace. Through the guidance of the Spirit, he gave me an unexpected blessing which challenged my way of thinking. The Lord admonished me to think about my own needs, wants, and desires. I was promised that as I did so, an unexpected chapter in my life would unfold that would bring me more joy and happiness than I had ever known. In the blessing, I was told that Heavenly Father loves me and I would be wrapped in the arms of His love.

Think about my own needs? That seemed like an impossible request. As a single mother of four kids I didn't know how to focus on my own desires or even recognize what they were. Was Heavenly Father saying that I needed to have another husband? There was no way I was going to put my children on another roller coaster ride of dating and relationships. I had firmly decided it would be selfish for me to date. My life would revolve around my kids until they were grown and that was final.

What did the blessing mean? I was confused.

My children were with their dad for the weekend. There were sections of their lives I knew nothing about—it was surreal. A court order and parenting plan spelled out when and for how long I would see my children for the rest of their childhood. Discouragement consumed me. Mindlessly, I went through the motions of cleaning the house and became exhausted. The dating workshop was the next day and that was the last place I wanted to be. I decided not to go.

Wandering into the bathroom, I turned on the bath water and undressed. Fatigue had taken its toll and within minutes I fell asleep in the tub. After five hours, I woke up and it was three in the morning. The water was freezing cold and both my mind and body were completely numb. In a semi-comatose state, I managed to pull myself out of the tub and dress. I collapsed into bed and decided to sleep forever.

Sleeping late felt good until I fully woke up. Then I remembered that the nightmare I just had was actually my present-life circumstances. After trying to stand up, I became exhausted and went back to bed, putting myself on house arrest. I tried to go back to sleep but kept having this nagging feeling that I should go to the dating workshop. *Oh no,* I countered that little voice in my head, *I'm not going to put on a show and act happy in front of eight hundred singles on the prowl. No way.*

I curled up in my covers and tried to go back to sleep—no such luck. By now it was ten o'clock. The workshop started at nine and it was a forty-five minute drive. *It's too late to go now, I'm home free,* I thought. Then came that feeling again, the same words kept coming into my mind—*go to the dating workshop.* I was getting really annoyed—I wasn't going and that was it.

During breakfast the feeling got stronger. By now, I'm screaming at the voice in my head saying, *stop it!* I could tell it was becoming an all-out war. After breakfast I realized I hadn't said my morning prayers, so I knelt down. During a discussion with God, I poured out my heart to Him, expressing all of my worries and concerns. I had one specific request—I wanted one day of pure joy. Each day of my life had been grueling for so long. After the prayer, I stayed on my knees and listened.

Again, I heard a voice in my head say, "Go to the dating workshop."

Finally, I realized this was a losing battle. For some strange reason, God wanted me to go to this lame workshop to learn how to *not* date. I tried to come up with any part of this workshop that would be worth going for. Suddenly, I remembered that dinner groups had been arranged in downtown Salt Lake City restaurants. After a long conversation with the Spirit, I surrendered.

I decided to go for the food.

What would I do with my hair? Because my life had felt so out of control I had been cutting my hair shorter and shorter and I hated it. Being a licensed beautician came with pros and cons. Even though I was good at giving other people haircuts, cutting the back of my own hair was difficult. That week I had chopped it until it was too late; the damage was done. At least my short hair and crazy haircut would make me less attractive. What a relief.

By the time I was on the freeway, I'd missed two hours of the workshop. *Whew.* When I arrived, the attendees were split up into age groups playing games. I was not in the mood to be social; *why was I here?* It took all of the mental tenacity I possessed to enter the fray. I don't remember ever feeling more physically and mentally exhausted. It was as if an unseen force was by my side, holding me up, and giving me the strength to walk into the room.

Somehow I found my group. They divided us up into two rows of men and women who were facing each other. We were instructed to ask get to know you questions. I found myself sitting in front of a pretty lady named Patti. She said, "You need to meet my brother, Michael. He's visiting from Oregon, and he is the nicest man in the world." I thought, *everybody's brother is the nicest man in the world. I have no interest in meeting your desperate brother.* She seemed nice enough, but soon the game ended and we went our separate ways.

After the games, the group met back together to hear the speaker. I saw Patti again and she invited me to sit by her. Soon her brother, Michael, appeared and we were introduced. He was handsome and seemed nice, but I wasn't there to meet anyone so I ignored him. We sat next to each other for two hours and my body language said it all. My legs and arms were crossed and I was turned as far away from him as possible. I could tell he was trying to get my attention and I wasn't interested, poor guy. Michael made a comment during a question and answer period that challenged the speaker. *Oh boy,* I thought, *he's a difficult one.* When the workshop ended, Michael kept trying to get my attention. He was persistent, I'd give him that.

The dinner groups were next and, of course, he wanted to join my group. I had reserved an extra spot, hoping my friend would come, but she didn't make it. Michael didn't have a ticket and acted like he was starving. Finally, he got my attention and I caved—I gave him my extra ticket. As we walked with our group to the restaurant, I was pleasantly surprised by how easy Michael was to talk to. It was like conversing with an old friend. I began to relax a little and enjoy myself.

Once inside the restaurant, Michael offered to buy me dinner. I told him that I hadn't dated much since my divorce, but if he wanted to take me on as his project he could. He beamed. We sat down, and I decided to order the most expensive thing on the menu and see how he liked that. Michael asked me what I wanted and I confidently ordered the high-end steak. He was thrilled; he said he loved a woman who liked meat.

My plan wasn't working.

At the dinner table, I sat back and observed how Michael interacted with the other men and women. I was actually impressed. He was totally focused on making everyone at the table feel comfortable. There was one man who was quite an intellectual and was spewing out all sorts of random facts. Michael asked him penetrating statistical questions that allowed him to shine. Another man was a rancher and Michael discussed with him the fascinating traits of cows. He had him eating out of his hands. A younger lady was a teacher and Michael related a relevant teaching experience he'd had with one of his children's teachers and made her feel great.

We enjoyed our dinner and he was thrilled that I was devouring my steak. Michael seemed genuinely amazed that I'd eaten the whole thing. Weird.

After dinner, we walked back to the conference center. Michael stepped out of the group and I tried to make a run for it. I asked some of the women if they wanted to go on a walk and they all said no. When Michael rejoined the group he asked, "Would you like to go on a walk?" Was this guy some sort of mind reader? He took me off guard, so I said yes.

As we started walking I concocted a plan to scare him off completely. I told Michael everything the instructor told us in workshop *not* to tell someone when you first meet. Without hesitation, I unloaded all of my baggage, describing in detail all of the difficult issues I was facing. He stopped, looked me in the eye, and said, "Those are just your circumstances, that's not who you are."

Floored by his response, I wondered, *who is this guy? Why isn't he running away?* My plan to get rid of him had backfired again but I was rather intrigued by his perspective. Obviously, he had gone through some difficult life experiences to be able to make such an insightful and sensitive comment. Michael shared some of the challenges he had faced being a single father for ten years. I, too, felt the same way about him. Those were his circumstances, but they didn't define who he was as a person. I really enjoyed our conversation and before I knew it, we had talked for over an hour.

We headed back to the main hall where the dance was ready to start. Quickly scoping out the room, I noticed there was a mentally challenged adult who was break dancing in the middle of the floor. As I observed some of the other adults rolling their eyes and acting irritated, I wondered how Michael would respond.

As we walked over to the young man, Michael's face lit up. With a big grin that showcased his dimple Michael said, "Wow, if only I could dance like him." He had total admiration and appreciation for this guy. With a twinkle in his eye, Michael gave him a huge compliment which encouraged even more complicated dance moves. His genuine and unexpected response to a disabled adult warmed my heart.

Michael and I quickly figured out that we were both better at slow dancing than fast, so we turned every song into a slow dance. Being with Michael felt like reconnecting with an old friend or relative, someone I had known for a long time and with whom I could completely be myself. Michael's genuine nature was quite disarming. It was refreshing to be with someone who appeared to be totally authentic. *Was this guy for real?*

When the dance ended, we met up with Patti and decided to go to the store. As we headed to the parking lot, Patti discovered I hadn't brought a coat. A few minutes later, she told me she was done with her brown leather jacket and wanted me to have it. At first, I didn't know how to respond. She took off her jacket and literally gave me the coat off her back. I didn't want her to be cold either but felt like it was important that I accept her gift. *Who were these people?*

Afterward, we got into our cars and I followed them to a gas station. Michael jumped out of his sister's car and immediately started pumping my gas, checking my oil, cleaning my windows, and checking the tire pressure. *Why was he being so helpful?* For a moment, I wondered if this was all a show or if he really was this nice. I was so confused. Before we said goodbye, he invited me to go with him to hear the Tabernacle Choir weekly broadcast the next morning. A choir concert sounded like a pretty safe date so I accepted. Michael hadn't rented a car so I would be picking him up. I would be in the driver's seat.

Instead of going home, I drove a shorter distance to my sister Kaylene's house to spend the night. On my way there, I realized that my plan to not date had backfired. *What was I thinking?* Suddenly, I felt scared. Sheer panic took over, and I thought about canceling our date. Michael lived in Oregon anyway; I would probably never see him again. What was the point in going? I must have gotten swept up in the momentum of the day. *No one* could be so genuinely kind and authentic. The reality of my life situation hit me hard and I was overcome with doubt.

I was at a fork in the road.

When I arrived at my sister's house reality hit me; hard. My life was a hot mess. I began a mental list of all of the reasons to cancel our date. I couldn't date someone living in another State—it was a logistical nightmare. We had seven kids between us. Utah was my home; I was born and raised there—and determined to stay. Almost all of my large and supportive extended family lived nearby. I couldn't uproot my children. It was unthinkable after all they had been through. From my perspective, neither I, nor my children, were ready for me to begin dating. My fears took over.

I decided to call Michael in the morning and cancel our date.

That night I had a vivid dream. In the dream I relived many experiences I had gone through in my past. But instead, I was shown how each experience would have played out differently if Michael were my husband. This dream literally went on all night long. I was shown how he would respond in hundreds of situations. It was an extraordinary dream.

When I woke up I was overwhelmed with gratitude. I knelt down and thanked my Heavenly Father for such a profound dream. I knew this experience was given to me as a spiritual gift from God. After living through many difficult scenarios in my past, Heavenly Father knew that I needed something spiritually compelling to convince me to go out with Michael. An unfamiliar feeling filled my mind and heart—I had forgotten what joy felt like.

Mile Marker Fifteen: Find Rest for Your Soul by Yoking Yourself with Christ

When Heavenly Father blessed me with such a powerful vision, I knew that God intimately understood my fears and was keenly aware of my broken heart. Without that extraordinary dream I would not have gone out with Michael. My heart wasn't capable of moving forward without such a profound, healing experience.

I continued to dedicate myself to the Lord and knew that He was traveling with me. Because of my weaknesses, my faith waxed and waned. One minute, I was dedicating myself to the Lord, the next minute, I was obsessing over my perceived failures. And guess what? It was alright. God sent me to a fallen world to practice having faith in Him and trusting in the Lord.

When a marriage fails, there are many frustrations from unmet expectations. Fear from the perceived judgments of an ex-spouse, children, and others can be paralyzing. A failed marriage doesn't mean we are failures. But Satan does an outstanding job of tempting us to feel that way. Often, I yoked myself to my fears and held on tight, allowing myself to feel powerless. I needed rest for my weary, divorced soul, and found this beautiful invitation:

"Come unto me, all ye that labour and are heavy laden, and I will give you *rest*. Take my yoke upon you, and learn of me; for I am meek and lowly in heart: and ye shall find rest unto your souls. For my yoke is easy, and my burden is light." (Mathew 11:28-29, emphasis added)

The Lord teaches us how to find rest by yoking ourselves with Him and learning about His meekness and the state of His heart. Through prayer and scripture study, the Lord *showed* me His generous heart. Then, at critical Mile Markers on my journey, He blessed me with carpool companions divinely inspired to teach me about me. With their help, I learned to reclaim my power by yoking myself with Christ. His yoke *is* easy and His burden *is* light. Through Him, my broken heart could finally *rest*. Easy yoke? Light burden? That sounded delicious to my soul.

As I began to yoke myself with the Savior I learned:

- *We were sent to a fallen world to practice becoming celestial.*

- *Most frustration comes from our thoughts about unmet expectations.*

- *I can lighten my load by yoking myself with Christ, the source of all power.*

Questions

In what ways might you feel better if you reminded yourself that being a mentally healthy divorce survivor or divorce observer takes practice? How would that kind of self-talk help you be gentler with yourself?

_____
_____
_____
_____
_____

What unmet expectations have you faced while dealing with your divorce or the divorce of someone you care about? Most frustration comes from our thoughts about unmet expectations. What expectations have you chosen to hang on to? Or to let go of?

_____
_____
_____
_____
_____

By yoking ourselves with Jesus Christ, our burdens can become light. Do your present burdens feel heavy or light? How can you yoke yourself with the Savior and allow Him to lighten your load?

_____
_____
_____
_____
_____

Chapter Sixteen

My New Carpool Companion: The Unexpected Trip

When I awakened from such a powerful dream, my heart was calm. All of my fears regarding Michael subsided—it was surreal. I knew the Lord was by my side, traveling with me, giving me the assurance I needed. My heart wasn't capable of moving forward without such a profound, healing experience. As I was getting ready to go on our date, Michael sent me a text that said, "Good morning, Sunshine." I had to admit he was rather charming. He had gorgeous green eyes, dark hair, and was quite handsome. As I drove to Patti's house to pick him up, I felt oddly peaceful. *What was God up to?*

Finding Sunshine

Michael had a way of putting me at ease. At the Tabernacle Choir broadcast, he put his arm around me. Surprisingly, I felt comforted and safe. When the choir sang, *God Be With You 'Till We Meet Again*, I pondered the words, wondering if I would ever see Michael again. But I was content to enjoy the moment. We walked around Temple Square and talked. After the concert, he invited me to Patti's for lunch and then to attend her church meetings.

As we drove to Patti's house, Michael told me he'd like to kiss me before the weekend was over—but there was another girl he had dated long distance. He was worried that she had stronger feelings for him than he had for her. He didn't want to hurt her so he probably wouldn't kiss me. He asked me how I felt about his dilemma. I said, "Terrible," with a wink and a grin.

At Patti's, we had a lovely lunch. It was fun to see where she lived. I learned that she was on the Primary General Board for the Church and worked for the Church professionally. She was quite an accomplished woman. She was putting on a presentation in Sunday school about the Church's new website, and she had to leave early to set up. We said our goodbyes. Suddenly, Michael and I were alone. There was an uncomfortable silence followed by an enormous grin that reached his eyes.

"May I kiss you?" Michael asked.

I paused, then said, "I just applied this weird tasting lip balm but if you want to risk it go ahead." He gave me a sweet kiss and then looked at me and said, "You're yummy."

Boy, was he likable!

During church, Michael put his arm around me again. Once more, I was filled with an overwhelming peace and comfort that I hadn't felt for a long time. I wrote him a note that told him about the blessing I had received earlier that week. I explained how Heavenly Father had promised to wrap me up in His arms. I said, "Michael, thank you for being His arms."

After church, we went back to Patti's house to visit and then it was time to say goodbye. I didn't know what the future would hold but I realized at that moment that Heavenly Father had answered my prayer in a profound way. I *had* experienced one day filled with pure joy. My comfort was tangible, I felt like I had been wrapped in the arms of God. We said goodbye, and then Michael gave me another short kiss. It had been a surprising weekend and I knew that regardless of what the future held I had a wonderful new friend.

Driving home and facing the reality of my life circumstances was tough. Dealing with significant health, financial, and parenting issues glared before me.

Several days passed without a word from Michael. Then came a text.

"Good morning, Sunshine."

I smiled from the inside out.

We bantered back and forth and set up a time to talk. Michael called later that night and I was surprised by how excited I was to hear from him. We talked every few days and tried to be transparent in our conversations about the reality of our lives. Michael had been a single parent of three kids for over a decade.

Michael's optimism was contagious. Was he really this positive, or was he just trying to impress me? We began having long talks on the phone about our lives, hopes, and dreams. Michael loved the Lord and it was apparent in our conversations. Slowly, I began to have feelings for him that were more than friendship. What was happening? This was *not* part of my plan. I could not imagine the difficulty of blending our families. Did I have that kind of faith?

I had made a solemn pledge that if I ever remarried it would be to someone with an incredible sense of humor. Not just mildly funny. My life had been so serious that I needed to start laughing again. One thing was for sure, Michael Rokus made me laugh. Not a slight giggle; we're talking belly laugh. Michael would break into funny monologues that were hysterical. It felt so good to laugh again; I had almost forgotten how.

Two months after I met Michael, I decided to fly to Oregon to see what his life was like. We had a wonderful visit and I attended his ward. Throughout the meetings, at least ten different people of all ages, both men and women, told me that Michael Rokus was a good man. He had a fan club of widows that sat on the back row. They had been diligently praying for over ten years that he would find a wife. They regaled me with stories of Michael's gallant acts of assisting them with their walkers, tire changing, cleaning their glasses, and fixing their plumbing.

Having a witness of Michael's character from all of those people was significant.

On the flight home, I thought seriously about a future with Michael. Things were progressing in our relationship, and I needed to ask myself some tough questions. How could I put my children through the adjustment of another marriage? Where would we live? Most of my siblings, nieces, nephews, parents, and friends lived in Utah. Michael's children, brother and sister-in-law, and parents lived in Oregon. Michael had a steady job as a building inspector for the county.

As our relationship continued, more phone calls and visits took place. I struggled with the prospect of leaving my life in Utah and moving to Oregon. Michael also considered moving to Utah. One day, I was in the temple fervently fasting and praying about our future. I opened the scriptures to the book of Ruth and immediately read the following verse:

"And Ruth said, Entreat me not to leave thee, or to return from following after thee: for whither thou goest, I will go: and where thou lodgest, I will lodge: thy people shall be my people, and thy God my God: Where thou diest, will I die, and there will I be buried: the Lord do so to me, and more also, if ought but death part thee and me." (Ruth 1:16-17)

After wrestling with the Spirit, coupled with ongoing fasting and prayer, I knew I had received an answer. I was to marry Michael and move my family to Oregon. It took some time for this unexpected revelation to settle into my bones. I was a Utah girl and had been surrounded by extended family members for most of my life. Could I submit to the Lord's will? Leaving my homeland for the man I loved would be difficult—did I have that much trust in the Lord?

Five months after we met, Michael proposed in the celestial room of the Bountiful, Utah, temple. With a prayer in my heart

I said, "Yes." That was the easy part. Making it happen was a different story. Accounting for the needs of seven children ages 11 to 21 was challenging. Michael had ongoing visitation with his three kids. My oldest son was on a mission. Both of my daughters were living with me in Utah. My fourteen-year-old son was living in Arizona with his dad. My oldest daughter was getting ready to finish her senior year in high school. It didn't seem right to uproot her at such a critical time. We needed inspiration.

My parents were still serving a mission in England and unable to attend. They had graciously offered to let me and my daughters live in their home for two years, and I had committed to maintain it. Michael and I fasted and prayed about our options. We decided to get married and then spend several weeks together in Oregon while my kids were in Arizona for their summer visitation with their dad. After their visit, Michael and I would live apart for nine months so my oldest daughter could finish her senior year of high school in Utah.

This plan would allow us to slowly blend our families. We would get together for holidays and special occasions. Building relationships with each other's children was difficult. We lived in three different States.

The morning of our wedding the children were struggling. Michael had been single for a decade and his children had not had to share him with a step-mother. My children were nervous about having a new step-father. Our upcoming marriage was a test of faith for all of us. Although my parents were unable to attend, and I greatly missed them, I was thrilled that all five of my siblings and my niece would be there to support us.

My Uncle Nathan and Aunt Carolyn surprised us and traveled from Utah for the wedding. Nathan was a temple sealer in the Salt Lake City, Utah, temple. Minutes before the ceremony, Michael and I were full of anxiety. At our request, Uncle Nathan gave us priesthood blessings which confirmed it was the Lord's will for us to be married—right then. We both received needed assurance. Michael and I pressed forward with renewed confidence and a huge leap of faith.

After a wonderful honeymoon cruise to Bermuda, reality hit us hard and fast. My oldest daughter had been fasting and praying about her life, and felt like she needed to finish her senior year in Arizona with her dad. This changed everything. It was difficult for me to accept her decision, but I trusted her ability to receive personal revelation. As a co-parent, I have always made an effort to be supportive of my children spending time with their father. I could have demanded she be with me and take the issue to court; instead, I respected her decision.

Michael and I needed to reevaluate our plan. I had committed to caring for my parent's home for another year and didn't know what to do. My friend, Pam, told me that her son had recently gotten engaged and the couple needed somewhere to live when they married. She spoke with him and his fiancé and they were thrilled about the prospect.

After more fasting and prayer, I decided to move to Oregon with my youngest daughter. Within three days, we had my parents' home rented out to Pam's son and his fiancé. Leaving Utah nine months sooner than planned was difficult. Soon we began packing and saying goodbye to family and friends. We would be leaving a way of life that was rich and meaningful.

We took a giant leap of faith into the unknown.

When we arrived in Oregon, I immediately felt comfortable. Because Michael is well loved, ward members and friends were welcoming and open. Oregon is breathtaking—I was moving to a beautiful place. My new home was within an hour and a half of stunning waterfalls and the coast. The clean air and beauty have been healing for my mind and heart.

Blending families has been full of ups and downs. It's been a learning curve and I have much to learn. I am truly blessed to be a mother and fiercely love my children. It's one of the most impossible loves to describe. A wise older friend told me, "As a step-parent, you are learning the meaning of divine love." I've grown to love my three bonus kids. I think about all seven of my children many times each day and have a prayer in my heart for each of them. They continue to teach me about divine love, joy, and patience.

They are my treasured traveling companions.

Life continues to have detours, but now I have another carpool companion by my side, my husband, Michael. The morning of our first date he called me Sunshine, but he is the light of my life. Michael is the most optimistic man I have ever known. He brings sunshine wherever he goes. His light comes from his faith in the Lord. He is always quick to give God credit with a grateful heart. Having such a sweet companion has been a compensatory blessing. Michael helps me see the world from a different perspective. Most importantly—he makes me laugh.

Regardless of marital status, true and lasting happiness only comes when Jesus Christ is our most important carpool companion. Each person's detour of divorce takes them down a different path. Some will remarry, others may not.

Every divorce experience can be a redemptive experience—when we allow it to be. Elder Jeffrey R. Holland was referring to Joseph Smith's imprisonment on false charges in the Liberty Jail when he describes how this is possible:

"The lessons of the winter of 1838–39 teach us that every experience can become a redemptive experience if we remain bonded to our Father in Heaven through that difficulty. These difficult lessons teach us that man's extremity is God's opportunity, and if we will be humble and faithful, if we will be believing and not curse God for our problems, He can turn the unfair and inhumane and debilitating prisons of our lives into temples—or at least into a circumstance that can bring comfort and revelation, divine companionship and peace." (Jeffrey R. Holland, "Lessons from Liberty Jail," *BYU Magazine*, Winter 2009)

Divorce experiences can be redemptive *when* we seek for the divine companionship of our Heavenly Father, and Jesus Christ, and remain bonded to them through the connective power of the Holy Ghost. Redemptive experiences are often shared with other travelers who have braved a similar road.

As we continue to appeal to the enabling power of the Atonement of Jesus Christ, and yield to the Spirit, over time the pain of divorce really will subside.

Mile Marker Sixteen: Divorce is Not God's Rejection; He is Redirecting Our Lives

My quest for personal peace has been a long and arduous journey. The trek has been filled with bumps in the road—and huge gigantic boulders. We often hear people say that they took a wrong turn and "accidentally" came across a great restaurant or a beautiful landmark. Some of the most spectacular scenery is discovered when our trek takes us off the beaten path.

When our new path doesn't include a spouse or contact with all of our children, the grief can be consuming. Imagining a scenic view ahead can seem impossible. The familiar paths we once traveled have detoured, and we are forced to discover new highways in order to survive.

God wants us to gain perspective. It is not free; it is purchased with a price—the cost is experience. Throughout our journey, we are given opportunities to walk a mile in someone else's shoes. Sometimes even the shoes of an ex-spouse. When we connect the Mile Markers of our past, by looking through the rear-view mirror, we can gain sincere empathy for others. Gleaning personalized perspective takes time, spiritual patience, and an abundance of heavenly help.

As I begin to revel in the deliciousness of my detour, my life has become full and rich in surprising ways. I am striving to tap into the Spirit, with a desire to become the woman I am destined to be. I will probably spend my whole life reminding myself that I don't have to be perfect to be loved. But now when I remind myself, I actually believe it.

My life's journey has taken me from a scared little girl, to a young woman, a wife, a mother, and a survivor of divorce. Heavenly Father has always been there for me with open arms, even when I wouldn't return His embrace. A stronger identity has come from believing I am His, a precious daughter of infinite worth. I am amazed at God's prolific love for me, an imperfect, divorced woman with much to learn. One thing I know for sure:

The detour of divorce is not God's rejection; He is redirecting our lives.

My journey has taught me that:

- *Spectacular scenery will be discovered when divorce takes us off the beaten path.*
- *Divorce gives us a unique opportunity to have empathy for others.*
- *Divorce is not God's rejection; He is redirecting our lives.*

Questions

What spectacular scenery and unique opportunities have you discovered as a direct result of your divorce detour or the difficult journey of a loved one? What special people have come into your life because of these experiences?

_____
_____
_____
_____
_____

What wisdom and perspective have you gained through your detour of divorce or the divorce of someone with whom you have an emotional connection? How have your experiences increased your compassion and empathy for others and yourself?

_____
_____
_____
_____
_____

How have you noticed God's redirection in your life? Where do you see yourself on your path of healing five years from now? What goals might help you arrive at your destination?

_____
_____
_____
_____
_____

Mile Marker Messages

Mile Marker One: Let the Savior Do His Job

Mile Marker Two: Give Way to the Rocky Road of Grief

Mile Marker Three: Seek Diagnostics and Repairs from the Master Mechanic

Mile Marker Four: Take the High Road

Mile Marker Five: Be a Driving Force in God's Miracles

Mile Marker Six: Keep Your Eyes Wide Open

Mile Marker Seven: The Road to Peace Begins with Agency

Mile Marker Eight: Slow Down and Yield to the Spirit

Mile Marker Nine: Let Christ Be Your Compass

Mile Marker Ten: Tune into Kindness

Mile Marker Eleven: The Lord's Light Drives Darkness Away

Mile Marker Twelve: Turn on the Headlights of Hope

Mile Marker Thirteen: Give Your Load to the Lord

Mile Marker Fourteen: Recognize the Signs of Depression and Take Action

Mile Marker Fifteen: Find Rest for Your Soul by Yoking Yourself with Christ

Mile Marker Sixteen: Divorce is Not God's Rejection; He is Redirecting Our Lives

Conclusion

Having a healthy marriage is not a basic human right. It is a gift that is dependent upon the willingness of both partners to see it through. But when a marriage ends in divorce, the grief can be earth-shattering. We are commanded not to judge, but sometimes Christians can be judgmental toward those who divorce.

I used to be one of those judgmental people.

Because of divorce, my heart has been opened, broken, and beaten down. I am still in the healing process; but I have made great progress. Ironically, many of the most extraordinary men and women I have ever known have been divorced; some more than once. The people I once judged are now some of my greatest mentors.

Learning to not judge those who have divorced is important for people of all faiths. I'm so grateful that I can continually repent, and for the enabling power of the Atonement of Jesus Christ which makes up the difference for all of my sins, weaknesses, and harsh judgments I have made in the past.

When we are willing to repent, the Holy Ghost will help purify our hearts. As we learn to feel the Savior's love, we are more likely to remember *who* we are and *whose* we are. We are literal spirit children of our Father in Heaven, Who loves us and will never leave us, especially when we wander. When this awakening of our identity begins to register in our hearts, we are on a path of healing.

When a marriage falls apart, it's tempting to blame God. Choosing to stay in a marriage takes the willingness of both parties. A deeper understanding of the principle of agency has helped to soften what I don't yet understand. Not every marriage will be successful, but God is there to help everyone affected by divorce. My journey has taught me a profound principle: The detour of divorce is not God's *rejection*, it is an opportunity for His *redirection*.

As drivers, when we discover a detour sign, there's always an alternate route. Suddenly, we find ourselves on a new road and we're disoriented. Most of us rely on our GPS to help us safely navigate our new surroundings.

While heading down the detour of divorce, our world, as we once knew it, begins to change in ways we never could have imagined. We are traveling down unpaved roads with potholes and vicious ruts. While trying to find our way, turning toward the Savior doesn't just happen automatically. We must purposefully invite Jesus Christ to join our carpool and turn the GPS over to Him. By trusting in Him to be our guide, He will direct us toward a beautiful rest stop, a place of healing, love, and beauty.

The Lord sees our potential, He is our Creator. He honors our journey and endorses our use of agency. As we connect the Mile Markers of our past, we have the opportunity to learn lessons along the way. Heavenly Father's perfect plan of happiness provides everything we need to rediscover wholeness.

When I invite Jesus Christ to be my most important carpool companion, I have confidence that I can put my worries to bed each night and wake up knowing that somehow, with the Lord as my guiding light, everything will eventually be alright. Holding onto this perspective takes time, patience, and a great deal of heavenly help.

I am learning that life is just life. A mortal experience—a test.

Many trials we encounter are difficult and full of darkness; they cause a lot of stress, sleeplessness, and worry. But this is only a test and we are not alone. Many divorce survivors truly have been victimized, but life is too short to hold onto a victim mentality. Light eventually comes from trusting in the Lord and traveling with Him. He will help guide us in our learning process. When we look through the rear-view mirror with eternal perspective, eventually peace will come.

Throughout my journey, Heavenly Father has blessed me with carpool companions who traveled with me and stayed by my side on some dark days. I will always be grateful for these treasured friends who were divinely inspired to teach me about me.

Carpooling with survivors provides us with opportunities to give others a lift. When we lighten the load of another, we may be making an atonement for one who is too weary to go the distance by themselves. We never know when someone simply can't go on alone. Lifting others helps us understand how the Savior lifts us.

When we let go of what we can't do and focus on what we can, that's when we're really living. Whether or not one remarries, there is joy to be found in our carpooling adventures, wherever they may lead. With our Savior by our side we *will* rise above the difficulty of our detours —and find joy in the journey.

Bibliography

1. Hebrews 10: 32, 36
2. Jacob 3:1
3. Joseph B. Wirthlin, "Come What May, and Love It," *Ensign*, Nov 2008, p. 28
4. Proverbs 3:5-6
5. Moroni 4:3
6. 2 Nephi 32:3
7. D&C 121:1
8. Job 13:15
9. 2 Nephi 4:27-28
10. Richard G. Scott, "To Heal the Shattering Consequences of Abuse," *Ensign*, May 2008, p. 42
11. Mormon Doctrine, Salt Lake City: Bookcraft, 1966, p. 771
12. Colleen C. Harrison, *He Did Deliver Me from Bondage*, Hyrum, Utah: Windhaven Publishing, 2002, p. A-3 & 4
13. Russell M. Nelson, "The Book of Mormon: What Would Your Life Be Like Without It?" Ensign, November 2017
14. Bruce D. Porter, "A Broken Heart and a Contrite Spirit," *Ensign*, November 2007, p. 32
15. Mathew 11:28-29
16. Ruth 1:16-17
17. Jeffrey R. Holland, "Lessons from Liberty Jail," *BYU Magazine*, Winter 2009

About the Author

Sheri Rokus grew up in Woods Cross, Utah, and began writing poems and music as a teenager. In 1988, she attended Ricks College, where she got engaged and soon married.

Sheri pursued a career as a beautician and was fascinated by the inspiring stories of her clients. When she divorced in 2002, she drove to a Christian bookstore looking for a book about divorce and left empty-handed. Sheri became passionate about writing the divorce experiences of others.

In 2011, Sheri left Utah to marry the man she loves. She moved to Roseburg, Oregon, where she went back to school. She received a communications certification and a degree from Umpqua Community College where she wrote for the journalism department. Sheri and Michael have a blended family of seven children and two grandchildren.

Surviving the Detour of Divorce, my Journey with Christ and my Carpool of Friends is Sheri's first book in her *Survive Your Detour* series.

Sheri is writing her second book titled, *Surviving the Detour of Anxiety and Depression*. This book shares Sheri's experiences with anxiety and depression, as well as her carpool of friends, who share their stories of searching for hope and healing when finding peace can feel impossible.

Sheri may be reached at www.SheriRokusAuthor.com.

www.ingramcontent.com/pod-product-compliance
Lightning Source LLC
LaVergne TN
LVHW041541070426
835507LV00011B/869